I0796954

Being Reasonable

Being Reasonable

The Case for a Misunderstood Virtue

KRISTA LAWLOR

HARVARD UNIVERSITY PRESS
Cambridge, Massachusetts
London, England
2026

Printed in the United States of America

First printing

EU GPSR Authorised Representative
LOGOS EUROPE, 9 rue Nicolas Poussin,
17000, LA ROCHELLE, France
E-mail: Contact@logoseurope.eu

Library of Congress Cataloging-in-Publication Data

Names: Lawlor, Krista author
Title: Being reasonable : the case for a misunderstood virtue / Krista Lawlor.
Description: Cambridge, Massachusetts : Harvard University Press, 2026. |
Includes bibliographical references and index.
Identifiers: LCCN 2025033257 (print) | LCCN 2025033258 (ebook) |
ISBN 9780674297470 cloth | ISBN 9780674304031 epub | ISBN 9780674304048 pdf
Subjects: LCSH: Decision making—Moral and ethical aspects | Practical reason |
Values—Social aspects | Belief and doubt | Judgment—Social aspects
Classification: LCC BJ1419 .L39 2026 (print) | LCC BJ1419 (ebook) |
DDC 303.3/72—dc23/eng/20250916
LC record available at https://lccn.loc.gov/2025033257
LC ebook record available at https://lccn.loc.gov/2025033258

Contents

Being Reasonable

Introduction

On Saturday, October 17, 1992, Yoshi Hattori, a sixteen-year-old Japanese exchange student, and his host family's sixteen-year-old son, Webb Haymaker, lost their way while looking for a Halloween party in a Louisiana suburb. Yoshi's costume was a white suit, imitating John Travolta in *Saturday Night Fever,* and Webb was dressed as an accident victim. Mistaking Rodney Peairs's house, which had a large "Happy Halloween" banner in the front yard, for the house where the party was, the boys rang Peairs's front doorbell. No one answered, but the boys heard window blinds clinking in the carport, and they walked toward the carport door. Rodney Peairs's wife, Bonnie, opened the door, and Webb started to say, "We're here for the party." Then Yoshi came around the corner and Bonnie screamed, slammed the carport door, and called to Peairs: "Get the gun!" Seeing how fearful she was, Peairs ran to the bedroom, grabbed his .44 magnum Smith & Wesson revolver, and headed for the carport. By the time Peairs reached the carport, Hattori and Webb had walked away from the house, back to the sidewalk about ten yards away. When Hattori saw Peairs, he began to walk back toward the carport calling out, "We're here for the party!" Webb, who saw the gun, called for him to come back, but Hattori, who was smiling and walking quickly, continued into the carport. Peairs yelled, "Freeze!" When Hattori did not heed this command, Peairs shot him in the chest from a distance of about five feet. Peairs then closed and locked the door, and Bonnie called 911. Hattori died on the way to the hospital.[1]

Professor of law Caroline Forell tells us that in his criminal trial, "No one disputed that Peairs was sincerely frightened and believed that deadly force was necessary." Also, no one disputed that Peairs had made a tragic mistake. Hattori was no threat. The only question for the jury, Forell tells us, "was whether Peairs's mistaken belief as to the necessity of using such force was reasonable."[2]

In a courtroom, jurors may get some brief guidance about how to understand the meaning of "reasonable," but they receive no definitions, no technical specifications. If you are a juror, the court asks you to use your ordinary understanding of reasonableness. This is true across the many areas of the law where a so-called reasonable person sets the standard for a wide range of behavior. The judge in Peairs's case simply instructed the jury that to acquit Peairs they had to find that he reasonably believed his life was in imminent danger and the only way to save himself was to kill.

Was Peairs's belief reasonable? Professor of law Cynthia Lee writes, "Reasonable minds can certainly disagree on this question . . . Arguably, the average Louisiana homeowner in Peairs's situation could have thought Hattori posed a very real threat of death. On the other hand, Peairs could have completely avoided the shooting tragedy by retreating into his house and locking the door" (Lee 2003, 168–69). Lee's remark suggests that one might judge Peairs's belief reasonable because the average Louisiana homeowner would have believed as he did. The idea that being reasonable is simply being average or typical is a tempting idea. Professor of philosophy Martha Nussbaum suggests that in practice the law often takes reasonableness to be a matter of *what is average or typical.*[3]

Is this what we mean by reasonable belief—that it is typical belief? Were this view correct, being reasonable would be a matter of conforming to prevailing social norms and practices. That would be troubling. After all, it is possible that prejudice infects the social practices of average or typical people. Given this troubling possibility, the call to "be reasonable" would take on a sinister undertone: *Be like members of the socially dominant class or else.*

Why is it tempting to say that a reasonable belief is a typical belief? One answer is that most people are reasonable in their beliefs most of the time, so it is a good rule of thumb to use what the average person would believe as a guide to what is reasonable to believe. A related reason is that typical beliefs often encode common wisdom tested over a long period of time.

Attractive as the idea is, thinking of a reasonable belief as a typical belief or a belief that conforms with social expectations is not, on reflection, the way to go. On reflection, we can see that the reasonable thing to believe may not be what everyone typically believes; similarly, the reasonable thing to do may not be what everyone does. Imagine a neighborhood, Fearful Terrace, where everyone believes that their lives are in danger whenever any foreigner approaches, no matter how calmly. In this fictional neighborhood the belief that any foreigner is an imminent deadly threat is entirely typical. Philosophers use fictions like this one to probe ideas, in much the same way the law uses so-called hypotheticals or physicists use thought experiments to test ideas. The fiction helps us see that a belief's being typical does not make it reasonable. A whole neighborhood, a whole state, or whole nation could have unreasonable beliefs.

The jury in Peairs's case deliberated for three and a half hours and returned with a unanimous "not guilty" verdict (Forell 2010, 1413–4). When the foreman read the verdict, the Louisiana courtroom erupted in cheers. In Japan, there was shock and disbelief. About these conflicting reactions, Forell says: "As the strong reactions on both sides demonstrate, what is reasonable depends on who is being asked." Here, too, we should pause: Is this how we should think about reasonableness? It is tempting to see disagreement about difficult cases and chalk it up to subjectivity in judgments of what is reasonable.[4] Disagreements about what is reasonable tempt us to think that reasonableness is a subjective quality, something in the eye of the beholder.

Were this view correct, though, reasonableness would be like the tastiness of beets—it all depends on who you ask. A little reflection shows that this "eye of the beholder" view cannot be right. As to the tastiness of beets, maybe it is right to say that if you find them tasty, then that is all it takes for them to be tasty. We cannot say the same about the reasonableness of a belief or an action; we cannot say that all it takes to be reasonable is to find one's own belief or action reasonable. We rightly hold that the residents of Fearful Terrace are unreasonable in their belief about foreigners. We all know people who think they are reasonable but are not. If there is something subjective about whether a belief is reasonable, we should not understand it along the lines of the "eye of the beholder" account.

We have now seen a couple of tempting mistakes about reasonableness. It seems to me that we make these mistakes because there is something indefinite about reasonableness. When I tell my teenage son, "Be home at a reasonable hour!" he dislikes it immensely. He finds "reasonable hour" frustratingly indeterminate. My son thinks I do have a specific hour in mind and if he is home beyond that hour, what he judges reasonable does not matter. Since I have the power in the situation—I am the parent, and I own the car—my judgment is what matters. My calling it an "unreasonable" hour only serves to mask the way my parental power controls his life. This line of thought leads to a cynical interpretation: "Reasonable" does not mean anything substantive, and its use is merely a power play, dressing up domination in the authoritative clothes of reason.

Were the cynical interpretation correct—that "reasonable" means nothing and is a rhetorical device to dignify raw power—then every use of "reasonable" would be suspect. But not every use is suspect. When Thomas Paine took up a pen and wrote *Common Sense*, criticizing the

British monarchy for its treatment of American colonists and arguing that reasonable people in England would back the American cause, he had a serious purpose—he was making a significant criticism of the monarchy. Or think about this example: The Fourth Amendment to the Constitution protects people from unreasonable searches and seizures by the government. This is a real protection. Reasonableness is a standard that ordinary citizens can wield against governmental overreach (so long as society is in other ways just).

There is a long history to the critical use of the idea of reasonableness. It is a useful tool. But we need to understand what the idea means if we are to use it to our benefit.

It is not only reasonable belief that we want to understand. Lots of things can be reasonable or unreasonable: fears and other emotions, guesses, actions, and people. What does it mean for a *person* to be reasonable? The law counts on you to know what it means, and demands that you be reasonable, not just in your beliefs. The law uses the "reasonable person standard" to judge self-defense, sexual harassment, and all kinds of negligence, from accidents to failed vasectomies, and many more things besides.

Outside of life and death decisions and the context of the courtroom, we depend on each other to be reasonable in daily life. Though rarely the stuff of personal ads ("reasonable person seeks same"), reasonableness is an ingredient that sustains relationships. Reasonable people are flexible; they are open-minded and ready to listen; they may have firm beliefs, and argue for them, but if they have made a mistake, they will admit it. Unreasonable people make unreasonable "asks"—a familiar topic among workers. (Here is a favorite example of mine, from a discussion board on *The most unreasonable thing an employer has asked you to do:* "When I was younger I worked for a sub-contractor who was a sloped roofer. He told me he didn't have workers insurance if I fell off the roof. He told me if I fell off the roof, he'd drive me to the hospital, and I was supposed to tell them I was hit by a car" [Reddit, n.d.].)

Reasonableness is one of the essential fluids in our social machine. In the United States, the stability of our liberal democracy—"liberal" not in the partisan sense, but in the sense of promoting individual freedom—depends on our reasonableness. Reasonableness is what makes it possible for people with diverse religious, moral, and metaphysical convictions to live together in a just and democratic society.[5] A reasonable person is both fair and respectful of deep differences in people's worldviews about what is right and wrong, the existence of God, and the nature of a good life.

A lot is at stake in our being reasonable: in our shared civic life, the ability to live together as equals on terms of mutual respect; in our private lives, the ability to live together in healthy relationships; and in our work lives, the ability to labor together in decent conditions. It is no exaggeration to say that what is at stake in our being reasonable is life as we know it—or at least life as we want it to be. Reasonableness is vital and under threat from forces that profit from our unreasonableness; but at the same time, it is an elusive quality. It is hard to say in so many words what it means to be reasonable. This elusiveness can lead to confusion, and even suspicion. We are in a curious position, a precarious one, even. We really need to understand our own reasonableness.

"What is it to be reasonable?" can sound like an odd question. Being reasonable is necessary equipment for adult life, and most of us are reasonable most of the time, so we have a lot of firsthand experience. Don't we already know what it is? Yes and no. We use the term competently. We're often reasonable. But the question I am asking is about the fundamental nature of reasonableness. Compare: We can say in so many words what it means to be generous or courageous. A generous person is ready to give more of something—money, time—than is necessary or expected; a courageous person does not shrink from bad things such as danger or pain. We understand the fundamental nature of courage and generosity. What can we say in a similarly concise way about what it takes to be reasonable?

It's tempting to look to the dictionary, but readers of the *Oxford English Dictionary* will find a list of diverse qualities: "Sensible, sane; having sound judgement, wise, prudent; fair, equitable; not asking for too much; willing to listen to or prepared to see reason." The diversity in this list just takes us back to our question: Why does a reasonable person have these diverse qualities? Something about the fundamental nature of reasonableness leads us to expect a reasonable person will be fair, equitable, sensible, and sane.

Being reasonable is a positive human trait, involving among other things being sensitive to another's situation, seeing their point of view, and being ready to see reason. As with other positive traits—say, being generous or courageous—the question of whether you possess or show the trait is not subjective, or in the eye of the beholder. And the idea of a reasonable person is not the idea of the average or typical person. When you count on your neighbor, or your boss, or your spouse to be reasonable, you are not counting on them to do what everyone typically does. You are counting on them to be sensitive to your situation, to be fair, to be ready to see reason, and so on. These qualities may not make your neighbor, boss, or spouse a typical member of society, but instead may make them stand out from the herd.

One natural idea is that "reasonable" is synonymous with "rational," and a reasonable person is just a rational person. Offhand, you might think that anything a reasonable person could do, a rational person could do, and vice versa. We can call this the "rationality hypothesis" about reasonableness: There is nothing more to being reasonable than being rational. (If you are convinced of the rationality hypothesis, then you think the question is whether Rodney Peairs's belief is rational, and this is all we need to ask ourselves about his case.) One theme of this book is that the rationality hypothesis is wrong: Being reasonable is not just a matter of being rational.

Against this hypothesis, here is a brief sketch of the view of reasonableness that I will argue for.

When you count on your neighbor, or your boss, or your spouse to be reasonable, you are counting on them to be sensitive to your situation, to be fair, to be ready to see reason, and so on. Why does a reasonable person have these qualities? We might start by saying that what is central to reasonableness is an ability to see other people's points of view. This is a good start, though only a start, first because *seeing a point of view* is a metaphor that needs explaining. Moreover, *seeing others' points of view* is far from the whole story: A reasonable person does not see others' points of view in a cold, calculating way—there are *positive social motives* that move a reasonable person. Also, a reasonable person does not try to see everything from another's point of view, but instead focuses on certain things. And a reasonable person is not a pushover, uncritically taking up the perspective of others: There are *critical abilities* involved in being a reasonable person. If you are a reasonable person there is a special way you see another's point of view.

We can start to understand this special way of seeing by stepping back. Developmental and comparative psychologist Michael Tomasello (2022) argues that early humans, several hundred thousand years ago, developed unique species-specific skills and social motivations that enabled collaborative activities such as hunting large game together. Tomasello has us imagine two early humans hunting an antelope; each has their own role, chaser and spearer. Both partners share a goal, and so they must coordinate their roles; this coordination requires that each partner understand the other's role and their perspective on the hunt. The spearer sees the chaser moving the antelope toward a stream, and so runs in a direction that anticipates the action from the chaser's perspective. Taking the perspective of her partner is key to her performing her role well. (Human children from an early age excel at perspective-taking. When chimpanzees are given a new role in a collaborative activity, they must learn it in the same way they learned their initial role, from scratch. Conversely, when young children are given a new role in a collaborative activity, they know immediately how to play, having learned from the start not only how to play their own role but their partner's role, too [Tomasello 2022, 97].) Now here's the crucial thing: The capacity to take up another person's perspective on a collaborative activity is not just about imagining their line of sight on something—the antelope, say. It's about identifying which things in a situation have importance or value. The spearer anticipates that the chaser will see the waterfall as an *obstacle*—a thing to avoid—and so expects he will head in a different direction, toward the box canyon that provides an *opportunity* for corralling the prey. Early humans were able to appraise the opportunities and obstacles in their environment, to discern value and disvalue, good things and bad things, and to do so from each other's point of view.

We are a cooperative species. We often work together, and when we do, we want the people we're working with to keep an eye on what matters. We want them to accurately track value. People can make mistakes, but being concerned to get it right about value and being reliable in tracking it—that, on my hypothesis, is the heart of reasonableness.

My hypothesis needs to be explained and defended. It will take several chapters to lay it out in full. Let me start by saying a bit more about seeing the value landscape.

Humans are evaluators. We have evolved to learn about and navigate a world filled with value and disvalue: obstacles and opportunities, appealing things and repulsive things. Some things matter a little, and other things matter a lot—the *pain* of a paper cut versus *peace* on earth. We judge and weigh value. What matters more, an *exciting* career move or *stability?* Having a *placid* relationship or being *honest?* If you stop for a minute and observe your own mind, you will find in your stream of consciousness a constant burble of evaluations. Maybe you are aware of a twinge of *discomfort* in your wrist, then a flash of concern about a friend who's *unwell,* a flicker of happiness about a *success* at work. From the moment we wake up, we constantly register good things and bad things in our environment. We continually map the landscape of value.

We are also social creatures. This world of complex and often competing value is a world we learn about and navigate together. In our frequent collaborations, we must take account of value as it appears to others as well as ourselves. For example, consider the owner of the roofing business who told his young employee that if he fell off a roof, he should lie about it, and that the owner would take him to the hospital, where he should tell everyone he was hit by a car. Was this reasonable? Details of the case matter: Suppose the owner fails to see or take account of several significant disadvantages (that is, "disvalues") in making his plan. First, the police would likely have the employee who lies file a report, and filing a false report in most places is a misdemeanor, in some places a felony; suppose the owner also fails to register that his plan for employees injured on the job had none of the guarantees that would come with a proper insurance policy (money for a hospital stay, and recuperation time). Might the owner be rational to play the system this way? Maybe. But he is not reasonable. He is getting it wrong about the landscape of value—a landscape that includes the very bad things that happen to others, not just the good thing that happens to him when he saves money on insurance premiums.[6] A reasonable person is concerned to register value and disvalue—all of it, including the value and disvalue others see.

This picture of a world of value and of reasonable people as reliable and cooperative evaluators is not meant to compete with a familiar picture of our physical world as composed of atoms and void, evolving in accord with physical laws. I will not try to answer the question of how value itself arises in such a world. My aim is to convince you that reasonableness is a distinctive human trait, drawing on a range of distinctive human capacities, fundamentally aimed at navigating the complex world of value. We have evolved to be reasonable, to reliably track value and disvalue, to weigh which things matter more than others, and to do so in ways that allow us to share our judgments about what is valuable. Just as we evolved to have thumbs for grasping things, tongues for speaking, and big brains for making inferences, we also evolved cognitive, emotional, and social capacities for tracking value together.

Why not just say reasonableness is rationality? There are competing definitions of rationality, none of which align perfectly with reasonableness. For instance, in his recent book *Rationality*, Steven Pinker suggests the following working definition: "The ability to use knowledge to attain goals."[7] It is common to think of rationality as involving capacities for making good inferences, both in pursuit of one's goals and in pursuit of understanding or knowledge. Our ability to make good inferences is impressive and important, but reasonableness goes beyond this definition of rationality. Cases like that of the roofer help to make this point. We use further powers, beyond inferential capacities, to track value and disvalue; we draw on an array of cognitive, emotional, and social capacities to map and navigate the complex world of value. We develop our sensibilities (a sense of humor tells us about what's *funny*, a sense of tact tells us about what's *appropriate*). We use our emotions (fear alerts us to *danger*, quiet contentment tells us about *homeostasis*). We use our judgment to decide what matters more than what. We are social creatures, and we argue with others and learn from them about value. (Someone just told me that *Slacker* is a great movie. Maybe I will disagree, but they are trying to help me find something of value.) We want to create maps of value that are sharable. To be sure, we could not do all this without being good at making inferences. So, reasonableness requires the use of our rational powers. Beyond rationality, our social emotional intelligence has as great a role as, if not even a greater role than, our inferential capacities in making us reasonable.

In the chapters that follow, I will explain and defend this view of reasonableness. In Chapters 1–4, I develop my account of the fundamental nature of reasonableness, starting with recent psychological studies that reveal differences in how we conceive of reasonableness and rationality. Then, investigating the function of reasonableness in the law and in our personal relationships, we see how being reasonable involves being able to think from another person's point of view. As I noted earlier, *point of view* is a metaphor. I unpack the metaphor this way: Your point of view is comprised of the things that matter to you—that is, value and disvalue as you see it. So, being reasonable involves being able to think about value and disvalue as another person would. I argue that this ability depends on a more general capacity to see the value landscape accurately.

"Hold on," you might say, "we disagree all the time about what is of value." Sometimes our disagreements are emotionally charged, and sometimes they seem irresoluble. (I say students protesting on campus is a good thing, and you think it is abhorrent. Our disagreement might get heated, and we might each despair of convincing the other.) What does it even mean to say that a reasonable person is concerned to accurately see the value landscape, given that value itself is so contested? In response, I show how reasonableness is a quality that helps us to communicate and usefully contest our value judgments. In Chapter 5, I uncover the cognitive and social cooperative dispositions that make it possible for us to have reasonable disagreements about value and to share our evaluative judgments. Reasonable people have distinctive dispositions—that is, inclinations or tendencies—to think and act cooperatively and to disagree productively. In Chapter 6, I apply what we have learned, and I build an account of reasonable emotion that gives a vital role to these same cooperative dispositions. Emotions are one of our most important tools for discovering value in our environment. Reasonable emotions help us learn about value together. Chapter 7 brings these morals to bear on reasonable belief. Getting it right about value is often a collective endeavor, and you can't get it right about value without getting it right about the facts. I return to the case of Rodney Peairs to apply what we have learned about reasonable belief.

If I am right, being reasonable is not just doing what people typically do, not just believing what people typically believe. Being reasonable is a substantial trait, a social, emotional, and cognitive achievement. In Chapters 8–11, we will take the reasonable person out into the wider world and see how being reasonable can make distinct contributions to our moral lives and our political institutions. We will see how being reasonable can help defuse polarized beliefs and polarized emotions. In the last chapter I reflect on the past and future of reasonableness. If we want a brighter future, we should appreciate the longstanding value being reasonable has had for our species and envision ways of fostering it.

1

Being Reasonable and Being Rational

Let's start with the differences between being reasonable and being rational. Any difference we discern will depend on how we understand what it means to be rational. We can start by looking at facts about our usage. How do we use the terms? Though we sometimes use "reasonable" and "rational" interchangeably, we also use the terms to describe significantly different qualities.

Dictionary definitions only take us so far in the quest for understanding the fundamental nature of a thing. But they can give a sense of differences in usage. The *Oxford English Dictionary* tells us about a difference in the etymology of the terms. The earliest use of both terms appears to be in the Middle English period (1150–1500). "Rational" derives partly from French (*rationel*) and partly from Latin (*ratiōnālis*), with several early senses gravitating around being *capable of reasoning* (a rational person) or being *an instance of good reasoning* (a rational argument). The *OED* tells us that "reasonable" derives from French (*resonable, raisonable, reesnable*) with early senses gravitating around *conforming to good sense, being just, fair, or impartial.* Today, although we sometimes use "reasonable" and "rational" interchangeably, our use tends to make a similar distinction, with "rational" pointing to reasoning and "reasonable" pointing to good sense and positive social qualities such as fairness.

Psychologists at the University of Waterloo have made studies exploring our contemporary usage. In a simple one-word association test, Igor Grossmann and his colleagues prompted people: "Describe someone who is rational" and "Describe someone who is reasonable." Some common themes showed up, with words used to describe both reasonable and rational people:

As Figure 1.1 shows, we are ready to describe both reasonable and rational people as calm, logical, and thoughtful. Intelligence is

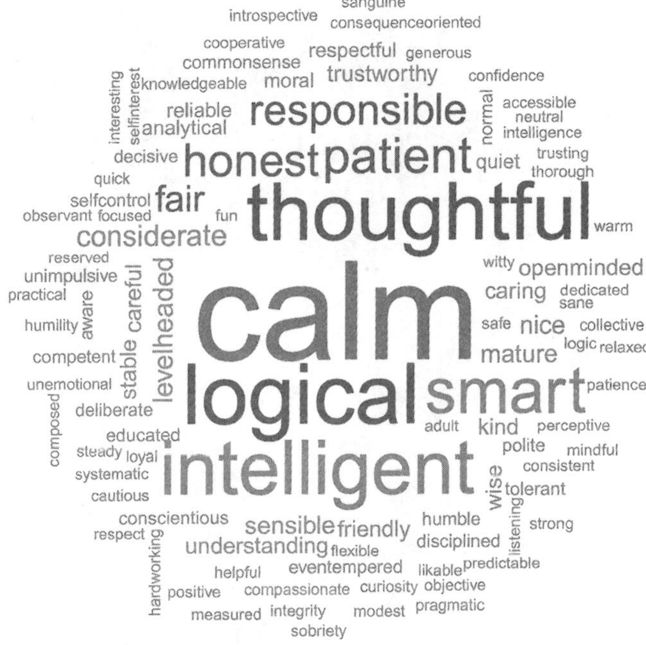

Figure 1.1 A word cloud diagram; words that appear more frequently in people's responses appear greater in size. *Credit:* Igor Grossmann, Richard P. Eibach, Jacklyn Koyama, and Qaisar B. Sahi, "Folk Standards of Sound Judgment: Rationality Versus Reasonableness," *Science Advances* 6, no. 2 (2020): figure 1A. CC BY 4.0.

another quality we expect of both reasonable and rational people (Grossmann et al. 2020, 2).

However, Grossmann found that we are more ready to describe a rational person as logical, smart, and unemotional, whereas we are more ready to describe a reasonable person as honest, kind, and fair. The experimenters sorted people's descriptions by those words more frequently used about a reasonable person (Figure 1.2, the top half

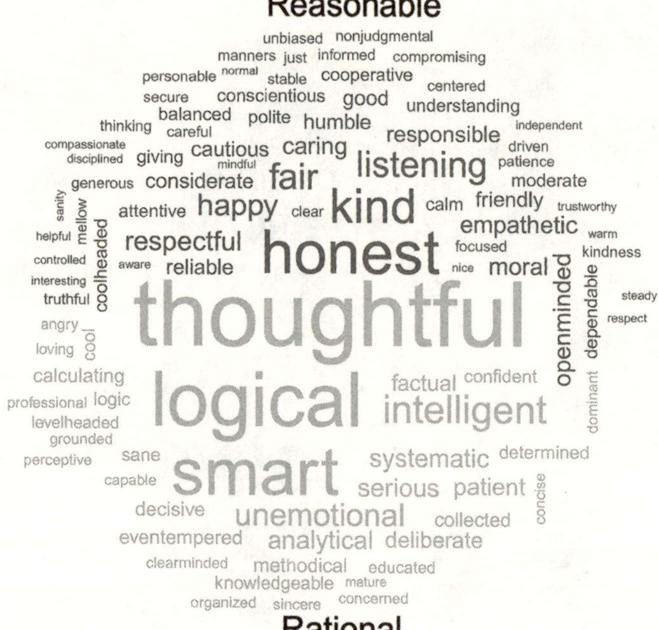

Figure 1.2 Words differentiating reasonable (darker text on top) from rational (lighter text on the bottom). Greater word size represents greater maximum deviation in a descriptor applied to the reasonable person versus the rational person. *Credit:* Igor Grossmann, Richard P. Eibach, Jacklyn Koyama, and Qaisar B. Sahi, "Folk Standards of Sound Judgment: Rationality Versus Reasonableness," *Science Advances* 6, no. 2 (2020): figure 1B. CC BY 4.0.

of the cloud diagram) and those words more frequently used to describe a rational person (Figure 1.2, the bottom half of the cloud diagram).

Rational people are more frequently described as "systematic," unemotional," and "analytical," while reasonable people are more frequently described as "empathetic," "respectful," and "listening."

A significant difference between our use of "reasonable" and "rational" shows itself in a game economists use to study decisions, known as the Dictator Game. Here's how to play. Person A is the Dictator and receives ten dollars. Person B is the Recipient and receives whatever portion of the ten dollars that remains after the Dictator decides how much to keep. Players do not negotiate, and they do not play multiple rounds. (Not much of a game, you might be thinking, and you'd be right, since A's outcome is up to them, and the whole play is over with A's decision.) Grossmann and his colleagues had people judge the players of the Dictator Game. They asked subjects: "What would be rational for Person A to do?" People answered that it would be rational for Person A to keep most of the money for themselves. "What would be reasonable for Person A to do?" they asked. Here, a sharp divergence: People said that it would be reasonable for Person A to make a fairer split.

Our linguistic usage reflects how we think. The Dictator Game study reveals that we expect quite different things of a reasonable person and a rational person. We expect generosity and fairness from a reasonable person. We expect prudent self-interest from a rational person. As Grossmann and his colleagues (2020, 5) summarize: "These results support the idea that people view rationality and reasonableness as distinct standards of judgmental competence . . ." In other words, we employ two different standards in assessing people's judgments and actions: we assess a Dictator's decision to give a fair amount by one standard, calling it a reasonable decision. We assess a Dictator's decision to keep more (even all) of the money for themselves by another standard, calling it a rational decision.

Let's look closer at the contrast between reasonableness and rationality as standards of judgment and behavior. First, a word of caution. Two starkly different figures occupy important roles in our culture's imagination: *Homo economicus*—an idealized figure who stalks through economics, the social sciences, and political theory; and the *reasonable person*—a familiar figure in the legal domain, where the "reasonable person standard" sets expectations for a wide range of our behavior. These personages exemplify some of the key differences between reasonableness and rationality, but we should be cautious about using them to draw the contrast between reasonableness and rationality.

Homo economicus chooses without fail to maximize his self-interest. Moreover, his behavior is beautifully predictable in mathematical terms. This is the whole point of his existence. As the Nobel laureate economist Paul Krugman (2007) tells us, "For most of the past two centuries, economic thinking has been dominated by the concept of *Homo economicus*. The hypothetical Economic Man knows what he wants; we can capture his preferences mathematically in terms of a 'utility function.' And his choices are driven by rational calculations about how to maximize that function." In other words, *Homo's* preferences are stable and consistent; he is not conflicted. He enjoys infinite capacities for calculating the value to him of various outcomes of his possible actions, and he is happy having these outcomes measured in terms of a single value (pleasure, say, or the satisfaction of his preferences) that his choice will bring him. He is single-minded in his choices, aiming always and only to maximize this single value.

It is easy to poke fun at this character. The economist Richard Thaler (2015) spoofs members of the species, calling them "Econs":

> No Econ would buy a larger portion of whatever will be served for dinner on Tuesday because he happens to be hungry when shopping on Sunday. . . . An Econ would not expect a gift on the day of the year in which she happened to get married, or be

> born. What difference do these arbitrary dates make? In fact, Econs would be perplexed by the idea of gifts. An Econ would know that cash is the best possible gift; it allows the recipient to buy whatever is optimal.

Krugman notes, "Nobody, not even Nobel-winning economists, really makes decisions this way." We could go further and say that *Homo* is not what most of us would call rational. When we call real people rational, we do not mean that they are utterly single-minded in the selfish pursuit of a single kind of good. A person so single-minded likely strikes us as suffering from psychopathology.

Defenders of *Homo economicus* complain that the spoof misunderstands him: *Homo* is an idealization. Scientists seeking to explain and predict complex phenomena use idealized models. Idealized models are simple representations of a complex reality. "As the joke goes, physics studies massless elephants on frictionless sandpaper," John Cochrane (2015) writes. Economists use the simple *Homo* to represent complex agents. "If you want to figure out the effect of prices on tomato demand," Cochrane explains, "the absurdly simplified rational maximizer approach gives a darn good answer."[1] Defenders of *Homo economicus* see it is a harmless idealization.

The economist Sam Bowles disagrees. He argues that using *Homo economicus* to model human economic activity is far from harmless. Laws and policies designed for *Homo economicus* can backfire when applied to real humans. Bowles (2016) discusses a frequently cited experiment in the Israeli city of Haifa, where some daycare centers instituted a fine for picking up children late. Surprisingly, at these centers, the number of late pickups grew to double the number of late pickups at centers that imposed no fine. Bowles explains that the fine "crowded out" ordinary ethical behavior, reducing people's ethical motivations to respect the teachers, by turning tardiness into a behavior with a simple monetary price. Bowles writes, "moral and other prosocial behavior would be affected—perhaps adversely—by incentive-based policies designed to harness self-interest" (2016, 21). Bowles is not against using incentives to encourage behavior that enhances the public good. He notes that some incentives work well. For instance, when Ireland instituted a very modest tax on plastic bags, use of the bags fell by 94 percent. Bowles suggests that the difference in the results of the Haifa experiment and the Irish plastic-bag tax owes to the way these incentives interacted with people's moral motives: The plastic-bag tax came out of a political process, with extensive public comment; and a publicity campaign accompanied the tax, showing the environmental damage of plastic bags. In Haifa, Bowles writes: "The fine seems to have said, 'Lateness is okay as long as you pay for it,' while in Ireland the message was something like, 'Don't trash the Emerald Isle!'" (2016, 203). According to Bowles, economists need to appreciate the ways incentives can erode our socially minded motives. Such motives interact with incentives and successful policies will combine the two with care. As we might say, successful policies will appeal to both the rational and the reasonable in us.

The reasonable person who appears in our legal system is more mysterious than *Homo economicus*. The reasonable person's behavior is not mathematically predictable. We lack formal models of how markets will behave if filled with reasonable people. The reasonable person in legal doctrine is concerned about others and careful in their actions; when they feel emotion, it is a sensible emotion, aimed at the right thing for the right reason and felt in the right proportion. Moreover, the reasonable person is unwilling to see everything they value reduced to one thing (pleasure, desire-satisfaction, well-being, or what have you). How reasonable would it be to value only your own well-being?

The reasonable person of the courts is also frequently spoofed:

> He is one who invariably looks where he is going, and is careful to examine the immediate foreground before he executes a leap or a bound; . . . who believes no gossip, nor repeats it, without

> firm basis for believing it to be true; . . . who in the way of business looks only for that narrow margin of profit which twelve men such as himself would reckon to be 'fair' . . . ; who uses nothing except in moderation, and even while he flogs his child is meditating only on the golden mean. Devoid, in short, of any human weakness . . . this excellent but odious character stands like a monument in our Courts of Justice, vainly appealing to his fellow citizens to order their lives after his own example. (Herbert 1935)[2]

This spoof is misleading, too, but not in the way the spoof of *Homo economicus* is misleading. John Gardner, philosopher of law, explains: "It is not the law's position that the reasonable person would always think, feel, and act reasonably all at once." When the law asks the question, "What would the reasonable person do here?" it is not asking us to consider what a perfect person would do. The reasonable person is not perfect. Rather, Gardner says, "She is reasonable in different respects, depending on what question the law is asking. A person who is always reasonable in all respects at once may be inconceivable" (Gardner 2019a, 3).

Gardner's observation means that the reasonable person who appears in our legal system is not an idealization but simply a turn of phrase. Gardner says it calls up a "character employed for the purposes of setting and communicating the law's requirements and expectations."[3] Using it is innocent enough, so long as we do not get confused and think of the reasonable person of the law as a fictional idealization like the ideal gas. The reasonable person is not some impossibly upright individual. The reasonable person is anyone who exhibits garden-variety reasonableness. When we ask about Rodney Peairs, "What would the reasonable person believe in his situation?" we are not asking, "what would someone devoid of any human weakness believe?" We are asking, "What would it be reasonable to believe in his situation?"

If being rational meant being like *Homo economicus*, the difference between reasonableness and rationality would be stark. But *Homo economicus* is an idealization, useful for theory-building and not what most of us would call rational. We should not try to understand the contrast between reasonableness and rationality by contrasting reasonable people with *Homo economicus*. Instead, we should try to understand the contrast between garden-variety rationality and garden-variety reasonableness.

What is this contrast? Let's focus on how differences between garden-variety reasonableness and garden-variety rationality show up in interactions between people. Moral philosopher Thomas Scanlon gives us this case:

> Suppose that we are negotiating about water rights in our county, and that there is one landowner who already controls most of the water in the vicinity. This person has no need for our cooperation. He can do as he pleases, and what he chooses to do will largely determine the outcome of the negotiations. Suppose also that while he is not ungenerous (he would probably provide water from his own wells for anyone who desperately needed it) he is extremely irritable and does not like to have the legitimacy of his position questioned. In such a situation, it would not be unreasonable for one of us to maintain that each person is entitled to at least a minimum supply of water . . . But it might not be rational to make this claim, since this is very likely to enrage the large landholder and lead to an outcome that is worse for almost everyone. (Scanlon 1998, 92)

It is not rational for us to press the landowner with demands. We can expect him to get angry and we won't get anywhere. But it would be reasonable for us to maintain that each of us is entitled to a minimum supply of water. We are all in need of water, and the landowner can see that. The landowner can rationally reject our claim should we press it. “But” Scanlon says, “he can’t reasonably reject the claims of others to water.”

Scanlon suggests that these judgments are intuitive, and they accord with how we ordinarily use the terms *rational* and *reasonable*. It might be rational for the landowner to refuse to share water with us. If the landowner has the goal of making his own farm as productive as can be, and that goal requires all the water in his well, then it is rational for him to keep all the water. He is just reasoning well to attain his goals. Similarly, if we have the goal of getting some water, it is rational for us not to press demands on an extremely irritable person. But why is it reasonable for us to maintain (or believe) that we are entitled to a minimum supply of water and unreasonable for the landowner to reject this claim? Scanlon takes it to be common sense, so let’s start by asking what we might commonsensically say. We might say that if the landowner is reasonable, he will see the situation from the point of view of others. He will see that his neighbors have basic human needs and that they are asking for no more than a minimum supply of water to meet those needs. If he is reasonable, these facts will strike him as needing to be balanced against his personal goals. He will be moved by these facts.[4] Scanlon’s case gives us a good instance of the contrast between garden-variety reasonableness and garden-variety rationality.

To see more about how the contrast between reasonableness and rationality shows itself in our usage, let’s consider another study of Grossmann’s. Grossmann investigated how people think a reasonable person would behave in a so-called Prisoner’s Dilemma situation, and how people think a rational person would behave. Here’s how the Prisoner’s Dilemma goes. The police catch you and your accomplice Bea as you break into the bank, and they are holding you in separate cells. For now, you are both refusing to talk. You each know that if you stay silent, you will only get a minor punishment, a small fine for trespassing. The district attorney has a plan to break your silence. He approaches each of you with an offer: “Confess, and if your accomplice stays silent, they will do hard time—ten years—and you will go free." Confessing, however, is not without its risks, as the DA goes on to explain: "I am offering each of you the same deal, and if you both take me up on my offer and confess, you will both do some time—two years." You are ready to brush him off, but he calls your attention to the fact that even if you both confess, it will not be as bad for you as it will be if you stay silent and Bea confesses. A lot speaks in favor of staying silent: If only you can both do so, you can both walk away with a minor punishment. But you cannot communicate with Bea and form a compact with her to keep quiet. You are alone in your cell, thinking, "Should I risk hard time in prison by keeping silent? Might Bea squeal and leave me in the lurch?" Bea worries along the same lines. And you figure as much: You realize that she is likely worrying that you will squeal and leave her with hard time. This line of thought tempts each of you to break your silence. (I invite the reader to consider what you would do.)

This so-called dilemma is more like a proper game than the Dictator Game, in that each person's choice affects the other person and both people can make choices. Here's how the payoffs of your options look from your point of view:

	Bea stays silent	**Bea confesses**
You stay silent	Small fine	10 years
You confess	Freedom	2 years

If you stay silent and Bea does too, then you get a light punishment. But if you stay silent and she confesses, then you have the rough end of the stick—ten years in prison. If you confess and Bea stays silent, you get a big reward: You walk free. But if you confess and she does too, then you both get a reduced punishment of two years, which is bad, though not as bad as the rough end. (Note: Theorists call staying silent the "cooperative" choice. Prisoners cannot strike any deals with each other, but silence is cooperative in the sense that you trust the other person.)

In discussing the Prisoner's Dilemma, game theorists and economists frequently draw a conclusion about what to do. They say such things as, "In this situation the best option for each player is to confess, no matter what the other player does." How is this best? It doesn't create the best possible outcome for the two of you taken together. Taken together, you do well to both stay silent. As some theorists explain it, "mutual cooperation leads to a higher payoff [for both of you taken together] than mutual defection, but it is not a 'safe' strategy" (Bravetti and Padilla 2018). Staying silent exposes you to the possibility of ending up with the least good outcome. Confessing gives you better outcomes whatever the other person does: If Bea stays silent, you clearly do better by confessing, because freedom is better than a small fine. And if Bea confesses, again you do better by confessing, because you get two years instead of ten.

Grossmann told people in the study a story like the one I just recounted about you and Bea. Then he asked them what they expected a rational person would choose to do—stay silent or confess. He also asked them what they expected a reasonable person would choose to do. People gave different answers about what they thought a rational person would do: Roughly half said a rational person would keep silent and half said a rational person would confess. But overwhelmingly people said that a reasonable person would keep silent.

When Grossmann had people think about a Prisoner's Dilemma iterated over two rounds, he found that people expected rational players to stay silent on the first round and confess on the second. (If you know you are going to play in the Prisoner's Dilemma twice against Bea, you may rationally choose to stay silent in the first round, only to confess on the second round, because it is the last time you'll interact.) But people expected a reasonable person to stay silent on both rounds. In other words, people expected a reasonable person to play in a cooperative spirit.

Grossmann sums up his finding about the iterated dilemma this way: "People view rationality and reasonableness as distinct standards of judgmental competence rather than merely opposite sides of the same evaluative (prosociality) dimension." In other words, it is not that we use "reasonable" to name a prosocial quality and "rational" to name an antisocial quality. A rational person will sometimes do the prosocial thing—staying silent on the first round of a game with multiple rounds is cooperative behavior. A rational person occasionally doing the cooperative thing does not erode the difference between reasonableness and rationality.

What does all this tell us about being reasonable? Is it just that reasonable people are happy to be suckers? No, no one is happy to be a sucker. Is it that you only see the benefits of cooperation if you are reasonable? Again, no—if you are rational, you can see these benefits too. The benefits are obvious. That is what makes the Prisoner's Dilemma a dilemma.

In real life we confront situations where we think, "If we both trust each other, things will work out well, but if I trust you, I might get hurt." What Grossmann's studies show is that in some cases, anyway, real people are quite ready to applaud the trusting decision, even if it is "unsafe." And we have a term for the trusting decision: *being reasonable.* We see rationality and reasonableness as "distinct standards of competence," distinct ways of reasoning well and making choices. We employ two quite different standards for assessing our decisions, and they are both legitimate.

What is the content of these two standards—what do they each ask of us? Take the notion of rationality that Steven Pinker articulates: "the ability to use knowledge to attain goals." Rationality is a capacity for making good inferences: you use your knowledge to reason about how to attain whatever goals you happen to have. As Pinker notes, everyone has goals, so everyone should want to be rational. There's nothing especially social-minded about being rational, understood along the lines Pinker suggests. If you happen to have goals that include making your society better, or making a particular joint plan go smoothly, then being rational will be in the service of reaching social goals. If you have antisocial goals, then being rational will be in the service of reaching antisocial goals.

Adopting this conception of rationality as inferential capacity makes the distinction between rationality and reasonableness clear. As Scanlon's water rights case shows us, we think a reasonable person engages in socially minded decision-making, recognizing the needs and interests of others, even to the point of modifying their own goals upon considering the needs of others. There's nothing in the inferential conception of rationality that requires recognizing the needs and interests of others.

Some philosophers feel this just shows that the inferential understanding of rationality is too narrow. Against this narrow conception, some maintain that rationality properly understood is deeply connected to moral reasoning, or reasoning about how to treat others. ("Moral rationalists," for instance, believe that rationality has a special role in discovering moral truths.) Still other philosophers argue for a broader conception of rationality without explicitly connecting it to morality. John Gardner and Timothy Macklem offer this pithy description of what it is to be rational:

> Properly understood, rationality is . . . simply the capacity and propensity to act (think, feel, etc.) only and always for undefeated reasons. . . . The rational person . . . is the person who fully exemplifies this capacity and propensity, and does so in her beliefs, emotions, attitudes, actions and so on. Wherever there are reasons, she does not defy their force. (2004, 474)

On Gardner and Macklem's view, rationality is the very general capacity of responding to reasons. ("Undefeated reasons" are roughly those reasons that survive after considering all the reasons available for and against a belief or action.) They further suggest that this is also a good, pithy description of what it is to be reasonable: Rationality is exactly the same as reasonableness.[5] Gardner and Macklem defend what we can call *the rationality hypothesis about reasonableness*. The hypothesis says that at a fundamental level, garden-variety rationality and garden-variety reasonableness are the same thing: a capacity for responding to reasons.

Defenders of the rationality hypothesis face some tough questions. It is not immediately clear how having undefeated reasons for one's beliefs, emotions, and attitudes explains one's being generous, empathetic, honest, and kind. And what are we to make of the data we have just seen? Grossmann's studies and Scanlon's landowner case show that we expect different decisions and behavior from reasonable people and rational people. In strategic situations of the sort represented by the Prisoner's Dilemma and the Dictator Game, we expect reasonable people to be more cooperative, trusting, and fair than rational people. This data counts against the rationality hypothesis, which collapses the distinction between being reasonable and being rational, leaving but one standard of sound decisions. We associate being reasonable with possessing a variety of prosocial personal qualities—being empathetic, honest, and kind—but we do not associate such qualities with being rational. How can we explain these facts if being reasonable is the same as being rational?

Maybe a defender of the rationality hypothesis could reply this way: "Our concept of rationality has become perverted; over time, with so much attention given to the idealized *Homo economicus*, people have come to think of rationality too narrowly. If people associate rationality with being self-interested, that's a mistake, owing to exposure to too much economic theory. And if your understanding of rationality is too narrow, then of course you'll imagine it is different from reasonableness."

The idea that we are confused about rationality is tricky to defend. You cannot appeal to our ordinary linguistic usage or our ordinary judgments about cases to defend it, because you hold these judgments to be infected with erroneous ideas about rationality. So how do you argue for the idea that we are so deeply confused, and that the fundamental nature of rationality is different than we take it to be? Moreover, you cannot blame modern economic theory for creating an illusory distinction between rationality and reasonableness. We began marking the distinction in our language long before modern economic theory introduced us to *Homo economicus*.

Just as we shouldn't take *Homo economicus* as the exemplar of rationality, we should also avoid a conception of rationality on which it is just being reasonable and vice versa. Our ordinary usage and our ordinary judgments about cases reflect significant differences between being rational and being reasonable.

Our culture pays relatively little attention to reasonableness, especially when compared to the attention lavished on morality and the virtues. Go to a bookstore and you can find texts on courage, perseverance, grit, and other virtues, with ancient and modern, religious and secular perspectives represented. Rationality—the flashy cousin of reasonableness—also gets heaps of attention, with books about its value and the flaws in reasoning that undermine it. One (possibly unintended) effect of this unequal attention is that it can produce an implicit assumption that rationality is the sole standard by which we might judge our beliefs, feelings, judgments, and decisions. I see this implicit assumption at work in my students, many of whom are deeply frustrated by the Prisoner's Dilemma. When I invite my students to play a Dilemma game in class, many of them say that they want to cooperate, but they tell me with regret that there's only one choice to make: confess and hope the other guy is a sucker. They assume that there is no alternative, credible standard of choice other than rationality. It seems to them that no other socially approved standard is available that makes sense of what they want to do. But there is another standard: that of reasonableness. The reasonable person is everywhere in the law. Our society puts its weight—in the form of coercive sanctions, fines, and jail time—behind reasonableness as a standard of belief, decision-making, and action.

Looking closer at the contrast between reasonableness and rationality as standards of judgment and behavior, we have collected hints about the fundamental nature of reasonableness. A reasonable person engages in socially minded decision-making, recognizes the needs and interests of others, and is willing to modify their own goals in considering those needs. Is the reasonable person simply selfless? No—it's reasonable to watch out for your own interests as you deal with others. When we think of a rational person, we are more likely to think of someone employing analytical skills and suppressing their emotions. When we think of a reasonable person, we are more likely to think about someone who exemplifies interpersonal sensitivity and fair dealing. Why is this? Ultimately, we want an explanation of what it is about being reasonable that makes a reasonable person naturally tend to be generous, empathetic, honest, and kind. A good account of reasonableness will help us make sense of the special connection between reasonableness and these socially minded qualities.

2

Reasonableness in the Law

On March 10, 1996, Rudy Stanko was driving at eighty-five miles per hour on Montana's Highway 24. A patrol officer pulled him over and cited him for failing to drive as required by Montana's traffic code, which read in part:

> A person operating or driving a vehicle of any character on a public highway of this state shall drive the vehicle in a careful and prudent manner and *at a rate of speed no greater than is reasonable and proper under the conditions* existing at the point of operation, taking into account the amount and character of traffic, condition of brakes, weight of vehicle, grade and width of highway, condition of surface, and freedom of obstruction to the view ahead.

Mr. Stanko appealed his citation, on the grounds that the state law was unconstitutionally vague: "It fails to give a motorist of ordinary intelligence fair notice of the speed at which he or she violates the law." His case went to Montana's supreme court, which found in his favor, holding that the traffic law was "void for vagueness" (*State of Montana*, 1998).[1]

One dissenting judge insisted there was nothing vague about the law, and that for forty-three years Montanans had no difficulty understanding it. Another dissenting judge stated: "The officer testified that at 85 miles per hour, there was no way for Stanko to stop in the event there had been an obstruction on the road beyond the crest of a hill. Operating a vehicle at 85 miles per hour on a two-lane highway with frost heaves, steep hills, and curves, where farm vehicles may unexpectedly appear, is not reasonable and proper under the conditions."

Montana later revised its traffic code. The code now specifies maximum speeds (eighty miles per hour at all times on an interstate highway outside an urbanized area of fifty thousand population or more, sixty-five miles per hour at all times in an urbanized area of fifty thousand population or more, seventy miles per hour on any other public highway during the daytime, sixty-five miles per hour during the nighttime, and twenty-five miles per hour in an urban district). But the law also continues to decree the need for reasonableness:

> Subject to the maximum speed limits set forth, a person shall operate a vehicle in a careful and prudent manner and at *a reduced rate of speed no greater than is reasonable* and prudent under the conditions existing at the point of operation, taking into account the amount and character of traffic, visibility, weather, and roadway conditions.

Despite the majority of the Montana Supreme Court being on record as not understanding what it means to drive reasonably, the legislature still saw fit to state its expectations for safe driving in terms of reasonableness. This was not perversity on the legislature's part—in many jurisdictions, traffic law provides specific, explicit speed limits in conjunction with a further requirement that one drive reasonably given the circumstances. There is good reason to add this requirement: Road conditions change in unanticipated ways and explicitly stated speed limits may be too high for bad conditions, but it's not feasible to provide further explicit speed limits for all such kinds of bad conditions. (How would this go? "If four inches of snow, go fifteen miles per hour, if six inches, go ten miles per hour, unless there is fog, in which case . . ."?) Requiring reasonableness from drivers is a time-honored way for the law to handle novel situations.

In the United States, laws invoking a *reasonable person standard* govern everything from alcohol sales to traffic law, from breach of contract to stalking. As Stanko's case shows, not everyone knows what it means to be reasonable. Even so, contrary to Mr. Stanko's example, you cannot use "I don't know what it means to be reasonable" as your defense. The law counts on each of us to know what it means to be reasonable. Or at least the law is prepared to treat us as if we knew what it means to be reasonable. Ignorance of the law is no excuse.

The reasonable person standard in Anglo-American law is pervasive, and the law does not bestow upon "reasonable" anything other than its ordinary meaning.[2] So, let us begin with a general overview of the use of the reasonable person standard.

Prior to the 1870s American courts treated injury law as a jumble of offenses with no general unifying principles to unite them. As legal historian G. E. White (2003, 14) tells us, "The crucial inquiry was . . . *whether something about the circumstances of the plaintiff's injury* compelled the defendant to pay the plaintiff damages. Tort liability was no more precise than that." So if your neighbor harmed you, you had to hire a lawyer who was familiar with a complicated pile of pleas and writs. (Writs are formal orders detailing specific forbidden acts.) Your lawyer could tell you if something about the circumstances of your injury was enough like a particular existing writ that a court might award you damages. Oliver Wendell Holmes, one of America's most important legal scholars, found this a sorry state of affairs. Holmes sought a general principle by which to judge harmful behavior. When to hold a defendant liable for the injury they cause? Holmes advocated for a reasonable person standard. His idea was simple: The difference between a person acting negligently and a person acting non-negligently is just the difference "between consequences which he was bound as a reasonable man to contemplate and those which he was not" (2009, 86).

A case illustrates Holmes's idea: In *Roe v. Ministry of Health*, an anesthetist administered an anesthetic by injection to two patients having minor operations. No one knew it at the time, but the glass ampoules containing the anesthetic had developed hairline cracks allowing them to become contaminated with a disinfecting fluid routinely used in the hospital. The patients suffered permanent paralysis after receiving the tainted anesthetic. The anesthetist didn't know that the ampoules could be compromised, and the court ruled that he was not negligent. To use Holmes's language: A reasonable person would not be bound to entertain the possibility of tainted anesthetic.

Explaining the need for the reasonable person standard, Holmes writes,

> When men live in society, a certain average of conduct, a sacrifice of individual peculiarities, is necessary to the general welfare. If for instance, a man is born hasty and is always having accidents and hurting himself or his neighbours, no doubt his congenital defects will be allowed for in the courts of Heaven, but his slips are no less troublesome to his neighbours than if they sprang from guilty neglect. His neighbours accordingly require him, at his proper peril, to come up to their standard, and the courts which they establish decline to take his personal equation into account. (Holmes 2009, 99)

Holmes here mentions the need to come up to one's neighbor's standard.[3] But we've seen that what is reasonable isn't necessarily what is typical among one's neighbors. Is Holmes himself mistaken about what it means to be reasonable? In Holmes's defense, he isn't defining reasonableness as whatever comes up to one's neighbor's standard. He is pointing out that being reasonable demands that we rise above our individual peculiarities. Even if we aren't typically careful, we still must be careful. As for defining reasonableness, there are few clues as to what exactly Holmes thinks it means to be reasonable. He assumes his audience knows.

In making *a reasonable person* the standard for negligent action, Holmes grabbed an idea—reasonableness—with a long history in English law.[4] Legal proceedings in early medieval Europe favored trial by ordeal—icy water, hot iron, and similar encouragements—to extract confessions. But by the twelfth century, courts began moving away from trial by ordeal to trial by jury. This was a major step forward for justice, but jurors were reluctant, having learned to fear passing judgment on others, since it could lead to eternal damnation for themselves. Consequently, jurors tended to err on the side of caution, taking any shred of doubt as a reason to find defendants not guilty. *Reasonable doubt* proved a clever solution to this unique problem. Judges coaxed jurors into making serious evaluations of their peers, encouraging them with the thought that so long as they found the defendant guilty beyond reasonable doubt, they could pass judgment without fear for their immortal souls.

What makes a doubt reasonable? By the seventeenth century, judges were explaining to jurors what it meant in terms borrowed from the philosophy of the scientific revolution. The basic idea in theories of evidence at the time was this: If after weighing all the evidence and considering all the particulars of the case, you had a "satisfied conscience," then you achieved "moral certainty"—a state of mind from which you could confidently act and pass judgment on others. Any doubts you might have after attaining moral certainty were set aside as idle, or unreasonable.[5] By Holmes's time, the idea of *reasonable doubt* had been in use for hundreds of years.

This small slice of history provides us some context for understanding the role of reasonableness in the law, but it does not provide us with a ready answer to our question about the fundamental nature of reasonableness. The notion of *reasonable doubt* comes packaged with the outmoded notions of *moral certainty* and *satisfied conscience*. What did "reasonable" mean to a juror in the seventeenth century's Popish Plot trials? What did Oliver Wendell Holmes have in mind when he suggested a reasonable person as the standard for negligence? To answer such questions, we would need to bring to bear all the interpretive energy and patience we must try to bring to bear now, in our own day, to figure out what we mean by "reasonable" in our use of the reasonable person standard. The historical task is no easier than our already challenging task. We can at least take away from this history a picture of reasonable deliberation about cases: A reasonable person considers all the particulars of the case before them and is careful about weighing all the evidence in an unbiased way. The seventeenth-century philosopher John Locke speaks of an "inner court" or tribunal in one's mind, in which one tests the arguments for and against a judgment. A reasonable person's inner court is well run.

Why doesn't the law just come out and say what it means to be reasonable? The answer, in part, owes to the fact that reasonableness is used as a standard (of behavior, judgment, feeling), and not as a rule. Laws encode both standards and rules. For instance, the Eighth Amendment to the U.S. Constitution sets some standards:

> Excessive bail shall not be required, nor excessive fines imposed, nor cruel and unusual punishments inflicted.

People seeking to abide by this law must use their own judgment about what counts as excessive bail, or cruel and unusual punishment, or inhuman and degrading treatment.[6] Article II of the U.S. Constitution, by contrast, lays down a rule: No person is eligible to be President who is less than thirty-five years old. A person seeking to abide by this law—say, a candidate deciding when to run for president—does not need to exercise their judgment to do as this law says. Knowing how old they are is enough.

Jeremy Waldron, a professor of law and philosophy, puts the contrast between standards and rules this way: "A standard is a norm that requires some evaluative judgment of the person who applies it, whereas a rule is a norm presented as the end product of evaluative judgments already made by the law-maker" (2023, 19). Laws that state standards demand that we use our own judgment about how to behave. Waldron recounts, "In New Zealand, where I learned to drive, there used to be things called 'Limited Speed Zones' where a sign alerted drivers to the variability of local circumstances and instructed them to proceed at a speed appropriate to the circumstances. Some jurisdictions just tell their drivers to proceed at a reasonable speed." Waldron points out that if the law says, "drive at a reasonable speed," it directs a person to apply "his practical reason to a problem to which the law draws his attention, and requires him to come up with and implement a solution." Waldron's point is that laws invoking the reasonable person standard treat people like self-governing adults. Compare a parent setting a curfew of 11 P.M. and a parent telling their teenager to be home at a reasonable hour. In the latter case, the parent encourages the teenager to think for themself. Similarly, the law encourages us to think for ourselves.

You might believe it would be better for laws to state rules telling people exactly what behavior the law requires. But that isn't always true. For example, should we replace the standard that says no cruel or unusual punishments with a list of punishments and say those are the cruel and unusual ones? If we do, we face a problem should someone invent a new punishment not on our list. If we think it cruel, we will have to revise our list, but we cannot hold the perpetrator guilty for violating a criminal law that didn't exist at the time of the offense.

The Supreme Court of Ohio explains, in defense of its own traffic laws, that the attempt to state explicit rules runs into a least common denominator problem:

> There is no place in all the public [roads] where a situation is not constantly changing from comparatively no traffic to a most congested traffic; from no foot travelers to a throng of them; from open and clear intersections, private drives, and street crossings, to those that are crowded. . . . (*State v. Schaeffer* 1917, 234–235)

If we adopt a rule stating a fixed speed limit, the limit will need to be safe for all the situations it governs. As the Ohio Supreme Court notes, this leads to trouble:

> If the rate of speed were definitely fixed, naturally it would have to be the minimum speed at which cars might be safely driven, because that speed would have to be a safeguard against every possible situation which would be perilous even at a speed of six or eight miles an hour.

The Supreme Court of Ohio wrote their explanation in 1917, so the speed they imagined for dangerous situations was quite slow—six or eight miles per hour—but their observation is a good one: The search for one fixed limit drives us to an overly conservative rule. By contrast, traffic law encoding a standard of reasonableness, the Ohio court explained, can "meet these varying situations, and impose upon the automobilist the duty of anticipating them and guarding against the dangers that arise out of them" (Quoted in Waldron 2010, 4). Rules aren't flexible, but standards are.

Preserving the flexibility of standards is one of the chief reasons that the law refuses to spell out exactly what it means to be reasonable (Hart 1997, 132–33). If our legal codes or our judges were to spell out in explicit terms what it means to be reasonable and what the reasonable person would do in any given situation, the law would take on a rule-like fixity. As legal theorist John Gardner (2001, 38) explains, the law remains flexible when individuals decide for themselves what is reasonable. Within the courtroom jurors decide what is reasonable, just as they decide other matters of fact.[7] Judges may give gentle guidance to jurors, and model jury instructions often emphasize a few things that might count as reasonable and things that might not; but the bottom-line refusal to specify what it means to be reasonable is essential to the proper functioning of the reasonable person standard.

The law needs to remain silent about what "reasonable" means. Gardner suggests that in consequence, the best we can say is that the reasonable person is *justified:*

> A reasonable action is a justified action, a reasonable belief is a justified belief, a reasonable fear is a justified fear, a reasonable measure of care is a justified measure of care, and so on. By the same token, the common law's reasonable person . . . is none other than a justified person, that is, a person who is justified in all those aspects of her life that properly call for justification. (Gardner 2001, 1)

Gardner uses "justified" with its ordinary meaning, "supported by reasons or evidence." Your belief that the cat is awake is justified by evidence: You hear it meow. Your feeding the cat is justified by reasons: He needs breakfast.

Gardner's proposed definition of the reasonable person is hard to fault—at least one doesn't find ready counterexamples. But the definition doesn't provide much insight into what it means to be reasonable. We want some explanation of why we expect a reasonable person to be honest, kind, empathetic, and good at listening. *Being justified* does not carry any clues to what links these qualities.

Even though the law must be cagey about what it means to be reasonable, we do not have to be cagey about it. We can seek a revealing, substantial account of the fundamental nature of reasonableness. How can attention to the law help us? The history of the notion of reasonableness in the law raises as many questions as it answers. (What is a "satisfied conscience"? What is "moral certainty"?) And the need for standards that keep the law flexible means you will not open a law textbook and find a succinct definition of "reasonable." If we are to learn about reasonableness from the law, we need to take a different tack. Our best bet is to look at cases. Especially cases where people fail to be reasonable.

Here is a case every law student learns: *Vaughan v. Menlove* (1837). Menlove, a farmer, made a haystack near the boundary of his property, and his neighbors were concerned that it posed a danger. It was well-known that hay ferments, and when improperly stacked, catches fire. The court records relate what happened with Menlove's haystack:

> During a period of five weeks, the Defendant was repeatedly warned of his peril . . . and being advised to take the rick down to avoid all danger, he said "he would chance it." He made an aperture or chimney through the rick; but in spite, or perhaps in consequence of this precaution, the rick at length burst into flames from the spontaneous heating of its materials; the flames communicated to the Defendant's barn and stables, and thence to the Plaintiff's cottages, which were entirely destroyed. (*Vaughan v. Menlove* 1837, section 10)

The judge in the case instructed the jury that their question should be whether Menlove exercised "such reasonable caution as a prudent man would have exercised." The court found Menlove guilty, but he appealed, challenging the court's standard of negligence.[8] His appeal argued that he was a person "not possessing the highest order of intelligence," and so the better standard by which to judge him was whether he acted to the best of his judgment. The appeals court firmly rejected Menlove's bid to use this subjective test of negligence, upholding "reasonable caution" as the appropriate standard for his behavior.

Law schools teach Menlove's case to illustrate the reasonable person standard. But there are just too many things wrong with Menlove's behavior for his case to be a good illustration of unreasonableness. Menlove takes significant risks with his own barn and stables; his precautionary measure (adding a chimney) seems contrary to common knowledge about how to build a haystack; and he doesn't listen to his neighbors—when told about the danger his stack presents, he says, "I'll chance it." With so many questionable decisions in play, how do we isolate the specific fault of unreasonableness in Menlove's actions? We could say he is unreasonable for each of these reasons. But that would mean saying it is unreasonable to take what look to us like significant risks over one's own belongings or well-being, and it is far from clear that this is true. Different people have different risk tolerance. Menlove's case is good for the purpose of highlighting the difference between a subjective ("I tried my best") standard and a more objective standard. But it is not a good, clear case for the purpose of identifying exactly what reasonableness is or answering the question why it should be the standard of behavior the law imposes.

Rudy Stanko's case is much better in this regard—it is easier to isolate what makes his behavior unreasonable. Stanko, unlike Menlove, is undoubtedly a capable person. In court he testified coherently about the condition of the road and his vehicle. His car—a 1996 Camaro—was new, and the brakes, tires, and steering were all in perfect condition. He had never had an accident. If Stanko wasn't driving reasonably, it owes to a distinctive failure, different from ignorance or basic incompetence. Stanko's failure, I suggest, is that he is not thinking about his driving from the point of view of anyone else. Rudy Stanko thought about how his driving looked from his point of view: The roadway was dry, the day was clear, and his vehicle was in good condition. How did his driving look from the point of view of a farmer, moving his livestock in an oversized truck across the highway? How did it look from the point of view of another driver, turning onto the highway from a side road, or approaching from the other side of a hill that obscured vision of the roadway ahead in both directions? To the farmer, or to the oncoming driver, Stanko's speed is reckless.

Stanko's unreasonableness, diagnosed the way I am suggesting, leads to this necessary condition on reasonableness: To be reasonable in one's actions, one must think about how one's actions look from the point of view of others.

We can bring this suggestion back to Menlove's case, to diagnose his failure. Among Menlove's many faults, his unreasonableness owes to his failure to think about his neighbors' point of view. His neighbors told him what they thought about the placement of his haystack, and he ignored them, saying "I'll chance it."

We should also add that a reasonable person does not just think about things from another's point of view, they also tend to act on what this exercise of thought reveals to them. A reasonable person tends to respond appropriately to what they learn upon thinking about their actions from the point of view of others. A reasonable person might fail to respond in circumstances beyond their control. A reasonable Menlove overcome with heat or exhaustion might not be able to move his haystack. Had Menlove been reasonable and in good physical condition, he would have built his stack elsewhere.

Jeremy Waldron's observation still holds: The reasonable person standard asks you to think for yourself, to use your own judgment about what counts as reasonable. But in judging for yourself what counts as reasonable, you must also think from the standpoint of others. The reasonable person standard does not instruct Menlove to allow his neighbor to answer the question of where to build his haystack; he must answer for himself the question, "Am I being sufficiently careful with this haystack?" He is the judge. But as the judge, he is not supposed to see things only from his own point of view, or to seek the satisfaction only of his own needs or his own interests. "Drive at a reasonable speed" doesn't mean "use your judgment about how fast you'd like to drive," it means "Use your judgment about how fast to drive given how other concerned parties might judge the matter."

Using one standard can deliver different results, depending on the situation. In *McManus v. Beckham* (2002) the McManus family, owners of a sports memorabilia shop, sought damages from the defendant, Victoria Beckham, who while shopping had spotted a display of photographs of her husband, the soccer star David Beckham. According to the McManus family, Beckham loudly proclaimed the autograph on the photos to be fake, telling three customers that the shop was in the habit of selling fakes and that they shouldn't buy anything from there. Newspapers picked up the story and the McManus family sued for damages. Beckham argued that she wasn't responsible for newspapers repeating her remarks. The court found her guilty of defamation, holding that a reasonable person in Beckham's position—a world-famous celebrity—could have foreseen that people would repeat her remarks and could have predicted that the shop's reputation would suffer as a consequence. Had you, as an ordinary member of the public, said what Beckham said and the newspapers reported it, you would be reasonable in not foreseeing that they would report this. Victoria Beckham failed to foresee what the reasonable person in her situation would foresee: that *her* saying the shop sold fakes would be newsworthy.

Looking at legal cases, we see a distinctive standard imposed on our behavior: A reasonable person is concerned to think about their actions from the point of view of others and act appropriately. This observation is a good start at uncovering the fundamental nature of reasonableness. With it, we can start to explain why we expect a reasonable person to be honest, kind, fair, and empathetic. Being reasonable requires being concerned about others' points of view. Fairness, empathy, and kindness all require sensitivity to others' points of view. We can also start to explain why a reasonable person engages in socially minded decision making, recognizing the needs and interests of others and possibly modifying their own goals. Why can't the landowner who controls most of the water in our county reasonably reject our claim for a minimal supply of water? Because if he is reasonable, he is concerned to evaluate his act of refusal not just from his point of view, but from our point of view.

The observation is just a start, though. It can't be the whole story. For one thing, the observation concerns our actions, and other things are reasonable, beyond our actions. Our beliefs can be reasonable or unreasonable, as can our thoughts, fears, expectations, "asks," and so on. What exactly makes Rodney Peairs's belief reasonable or unreasonable? What makes a fear reasonable? It is not clear how thinking from another person's point of view has much to do with belief or fear.

At least we have what seems like a necessary condition for being reasonable. If you can't or won't think about your actions from the point of view of others, you're not reasonable. We can start to dig further into what it means to be reasonable by concentrating on what it means to think from the point of view of others. "Point of view" is a metaphor. A person's "point of view" might refer to their visual perspective: "a point of view shot" in the movies is a shot that puts you in the character's shoes so that your visual experience is their visual experience. It might also refer to their opinions, their values, or what they know. Let's delve into how a reasonable person sees another person's point of view.

3

Reasonableness in Person

Bestselling author Ann Patchett has flown a lot. She often joins her husband, Karl, in his single-engine plane, hopping from their home base in Nashville to destinations around the southeast. Her 2021 essay "Flight Plan" opens with a story of one particularly unnerving adventure early in her relationship with Karl. On a fishing trip in Alaska, every morning they flew by pontoon plane deeper into the wilderness. The pilot learned that Karl was plane-crazy, and one day suggested Karl take the controls. Never having landed on water, Karl got some last-minute instruction. Ann recounts what happened next: "Karl took off toward the shore, and then we lifted off the lake, flew past the mountains, through the clouds, around the blue sky, back through the clouds and past the mountains, then nose up, plane down, smack into the lake. The pilot offered Karl some pointers, some praise. There was a quick discussion of how the landing could be improved, and then we were off again, a tighter circle, greater speed, straight up, lake-mountain-cloud-blue-cloud-mountain-lake, the nose up as we came down. The jolt was harder this time—I felt it in my spine—but before I could fully register my relief we were up again: a carnival ride for which no one bothered to take the tickets."

Is Karl being unreasonable, taking this flight lesson with Ann aboard? There are many pressing questions we might have about Karl's behavior—is he being selfish, foolhardy, or irresponsible? I want to focus on whether he is being reasonable. A reasonable person thinks about what they are doing from other people's points of view. So, if Karl were reasonable, he would think about things from Ann's point of view. Compare the legal case where Menlove burned down his neighbor's cottages: Had Menlove been reasonable, he would have been thinking about his neighbor's point of view when he built his haystack.

We need a better understanding of what it means to think from another person's point of view. What exactly is *a point of view?*

We often talk about a person's having a point of view, and about people differing in their points of view. (The question-and-answer website Quora hosts lively discussions of such questions as "How can you make someone see your point of view?" and "How do you know when to stop trying to make someone see your point of view?") When we talk about seeing a person's point of view, we are using a metaphor. If someone pleads with another person, "See this from my point of view," what is he asking the other person to do?

Let's think about Ann's case. Specific things matter to Ann about the flight lesson. She sees it as *dangerous*, *extremely physically uncomfortable*, and *unnecessary*. These are the things that matter to Ann about it, and they are the things she wants Karl to think about. So, we can say that Ann's point of view on the flight lesson is defined by the things that matter to her about it (that it is *dangerous*, *extremely physically uncomfortable*, and *unnecessary*). Karl has a different point of view about the lesson. What matters to Karl is that it is *fun*, and it is *a great chance to learn a new piloting skill*. So, we can say, seeing another person's point of view involves understanding what matters to them. It involves knowing their concerns.

Now we can quickly see that to be reasonable you need to do more than think about your action from the other person's point of view: a con man can do that. In running his billion-dollar Ponzi scheme, Bernie Madoff knew that his *trustworthiness* would matter to his victims. He knew they would be concerned about that. So he duped his own family—his own brother and his own sons were on his client list—to help create an impression of his trustworthiness among new investors. Who would steal from their own family? Madoff was very insightful about his victims' concerns (Huang 2013). He could think from their point of view. In Karl and Ann's case, if the copilot had an extortionist streak, he would think about what matters to Ann, and then he would ask her how much she'd be willing to pay him to land the plane.

What more do we have to do to be reasonable than think from another person's point of view? We might say that you have to think from their point of view in a particular way. If you are reasonable, you do not just happen to think about what matters to others; you want to understand what matters to them. But that is also true of a con man or a grifter. So we might add: If you are reasonable, that something matters to another person also matters to you. Suppose Ann is concerned that the lesson could easily kill them all. That Ann is concerned in this way is itself something that matters to Karl if he is reasonable. But again, having the concerns of others matter to you is not enough to separate the reasonable person from the grifter. Bernie Madoff sees what matters to his victims: They are concerned to maximize the return on their investments. That they're concerned matters to Madoff—it creates an opportunity for him to exploit them. So, we still need to say more about the special way a reasonable person takes account of the viewpoint of others.

One thing Bernie Madoff knew very well was that his victims were concerned about maximizing their returns, but Madoff himself didn't act as if maximizing their returns mattered at all. That they *had* this concern mattered to him—it is what allowed him to exploit them. But he didn't see their maximizing their returns as actually mattering. This is a difference between the grifter and the reasonable person. If you are reasonable, you think about the other person's point of view in a special way, namely, you are open to the possibility that what matters to the other person does matter. You are open to the possibility that what matters to the other is important.

Madoff was not open to the possibility that it mattered to maximize returns to his clients. He never gave that a thought. If he had been open to its mattering, he might have ended up feeling pressure to drop his Ponzi scheme and to earn his clients a real return. And that would have meant a big overhaul of what mattered to him. Being open-minded about what actually matters is a hallmark of reasonableness. Such open-mindedness can cause changes in what matters to you. If you are reasonable, encountering other people and their concerns can change your own concerns. Being reasonable involves being ready to change your own concerns. It means being open to changes in your own point of view.

A reasonable person does not uncritically accept changes in their point of view. Openness has its limits. Imagine a pathological case where a person is concerned about things that obviously do not matter. Imagine that Warren compulsively turns on radios. If Warren wants to turn on all the radios he sees, maybe what matters to him is clear enough, but what matters to him—turning on every radio—does not actually matter. If you care about Warren, *that* he has this concern matters to you—you might try to help him in some way—but what matters to him is something that does not matter. One needn't be open to changing one's point of view in such cases.

Being open to another person's point of view is something we do carefully. Imagine Karl is open to the possibility that Ann's point of view reveals something that he has not seen about the danger of the flight lesson. He does not have to just switch over to having Ann's point of view. He can instead decide that Ann's fear, while understandable—she is new to flying after all—fails to accurately register the danger of the flight lesson. Or imagine Karl disagrees with Ann about whether physical discomfort is anything to be concerned about. He believes that physical discomfort does not matter much at all, and that most people set too much stock in physical comfort. Ann believes it does matter, and quite a lot. Here their disagreement goes deeper than just disagreeing about what matters to them; they disagree about what matters, period. They have different beliefs about the importance of comfort. Now Karl needs to use his judgment, critically assessing whether to change his beliefs about discomfort. If Karl is reasonable, he is open to the possibility that he is wrong, and that physical discomfort does matter, more than he had believed; but he does not need to ultimately be convinced that it does. It is one thing to be open to the possibility that someone else's concern tracks what is important, and another thing to be ultimately convinced that they're right.

If Karl is reasonable, he will be open-minded: he'll be ready to think that what Ann is concerned about might matter and so he might overhaul what matters to him. But he will also be critically minded: he'll maintain his own sense of what matters—that the physical discomfort of the lesson is not a big deal—and try to judge what really does matter in the situation at hand. This demand for one to use one's judgment about the correctness or appropriateness of the other's concerns is also part of what it takes to be reasonable.

So, a reasonable person is both open-minded and critically minded. Why? At bottom, because a reasonable person wants to get it right about what really matters. If one isn't concerned to assess what really matters, one might be not just closed-minded about others' concerns but even dogmatic in one's viewpoint. If one isn't concerned to assess what really matters, one's openness to changing one's point of view might amount to fickleness. To be reasonable, one can be neither dogmatic nor fickle.

Human concerns take complicated forms, and being reasonable can require one to be responsive to concerns one has never before recognized. Here is a case where what matters to one person is novel for another:

> Assaf and his sister are concerned about their elderly father. What level of care does he need? Should he have home care or move to an assisted living facility? Assaf wants to be on the same page as his sister. But his sister never talks about their dad, and she makes significant decisions about their dad's healthcare on her own, without consulting Assaf. Even though his sister makes decisions that Assaf agrees with, Assaf finds her unreasonable because she never consults with him.

Assaf and his sister agree about what matters regarding their dad's care. They both want what's best for him, and they tend to think the same things about what's best. Assaf wants to discuss decisions and jointly plan their dad's care. His sister never listens to his pleas on this score. What makes her unreasonable is not that she prefers unilateral decision-making. What makes her unreasonable is that she does not so much as entertain the possibility that being on the same page with Assaf matters.

If Assaf's sister were reasonable, she would be open to the importance of communicating about decisions. She never before considered whether such things mattered, but if she were reasonable, she would be open to learning about what is to her a very new thing to be concerned about. Being reasonable means being open to learning about what matters.

A terminological note: When a person says, for instance, "being on the same page matters," we can take them to mean "being on the same page is valuable." People often use the phrases "it's valuable" and "it matters" interchangeably, and we will follow this ordinary usage. When Assaf says "being consulted matters to me," we can take him to mean "I value being consulted." And when we say Assaf has a concern about being consulted, we mean being consulted matters to him; it's a thing he values.

Summing up what we have seen so far: A reasonable person thinks about their actions from another person's point of view, and does so in a way that combines being open-minded and being critically minded. Reasonableness is a neat balancing act. Unlike the con man, a reasonable person is genuinely open to the possibility that what matters to others actually matters, that it is actually of value. So, a reasonable person is open to change in their own point of view. Unlike a fickle person, or a person who easily falls under the sway of others, a reasonable person is also critically minded; they question whether what matters to others actually matters, whether it is actually of value. If you are a reasonable person, there is a special way you see another's point of view: You are concerned to see what matters to them, with an eye to what really matters.

This is far from the caricature of reasonableness as a cold and inflexible quality that disposes a person to scold others about conforming to existing social norms, or to badger others into agreement. The grumpy and unbending person who says, "Be reasonable!" meaning, "See things my way or else!" is anything but reasonable. Reasonableness leaves you open to others' concerns and may change you.

As we've already noted, a reasonable person does not just think in an open-minded way. They also tend to act on what this exercise of thought reveals to them. A reasonable person tends to respond appropriately to the things that matter in any given situation. In Karl's case, staying alive to fish another day matters more than acquiring a cool new skill, and a reasonable person doesn't just see this, but acts on it too. Going forward, I will take this point about reasonableness as a given: A reasonable person doesn't just understand what matters, but acts on that understanding.

Returning to the case of Ann and Karl, someone might object: "But Ann apparently did not say anything to alert Karl to her concerns. If that's the case, Karl is being thoughtless, certainly, but he is not unreasonable; he is only unreasonable if Ann asks him to stop the lesson and he refuses." The objection raises questions about how much a reasonable person must know without being told about others' concerns, and about the difference between reasonableness and thoughtfulness. Let's start with the latter question—what distinguishes reasonableness from thoughtfulness?

The word "thoughtful" has many different senses. Psychologists use it to mean everything from *having well-reasoned beliefs*, to having *thoughts about your thoughts*, to *thinking lots and lots.* (Psychologists study the "thoughtfulness heuristic" that says, roughly, if you have thought about something for a long time, then you've probably reached a correct judgment.) The subjects in Grossmann's experiments use "thoughtful" to describe both reasonable and rational people: thoughtfulness is a shared quality of reasonable and rational people (Chapter 1, Figure 1.1). But subjects also associate "thoughtful" more with a rational person than a reasonable person (Chapter 1, Figure 1.2). This combination of results likely owes to "thoughtful" having two meanings or senses: it can mean *considerate,* and it can also mean *prone to thinking hard.* These two senses—denoting a socially minded quality and a more individualistic quality—sit on opposite sides of the divide between the reasonable and rational.

We do not ordinarily take it that a considerate person is prone to thinking thoughts about their thoughts or thinking lots and lots. A considerate person thinks, for sure, but not necessarily about their own thoughts; a considerate person thinks as much as they need to, which is sometimes not a lot. Ann Patchett in her essay says of Karl that he was "honest about everything, which should not be confused with being thoughtful about everything." The sense of "thoughtful" that she has in mind here has to do with being considerate.

What does it take to be thoughtful in the sense of being considerate? What might Ann want from Karl specifically, in wanting him to be more considerate? She might want him to think about what matters to her before she tells him. If Karl were thoughtful, he would try to be proactive in seeing Ann's point of view: before taking the controls in the cockpit, he would check in, to see if his plan of action looks okay from her point of view: "Wow, the chance to learn how to land a pontoon plane! But Ann might not like that." A readiness to act is also important. Karl wouldn't be considerate if he understood exactly what mattered to Ann and did nothing.

Thoughtfulness—again, in the sense of being considerate—seems to share with reasonableness an openness to another person's point of view, but it is distinct from reasonableness, too. A key difference between them is this: You can be considerate or thoughtful of others without thinking about whether what matters to them actually matters. Suppose your neighbor collects garden gnomes. You give him a new one for his collection—very considerate, very thoughtful! You do not have to be open to the possibility that collecting gnomes is a good thing. If fact, you probably do well to suppress critical consideration of whether what matters to your neighbor is of any value, insofar as you aim to make a thoughtful gesture. You can be thoughtful without being open-minded or critically minded in the way a reasonable person must be.

Does that mean no critical thinking is involved in thoughtfulness? No. For instance, it is not thoughtful to give an addict their drug of choice—that is *enabling,* not *being thoughtful.* You must engage in some critical thinking if you are to be a thoughtful person and not an enabler. As with reasonableness, the critical thinking required focuses on what matters to the addict. But it is not the same critical evaluation that reasonableness requires. Being reasonable requires an openness to the possibility that what matters to another is really of value; this means being open to changes in what matters to oneself. Consequently, reasonableness requires serious critical assessment of whether what matters to the other person really matters. Being thoughtful, by contrast, does not require an openness to the possibility that what matters to another person is of any value. Thoughtfulness does not necessarily leave you open to a change in your own practical reasoning or a change in your concerns. Instead, thoughtfulness requires assessing the impact and consequences of the other person getting what they want or attaining what matters to them. If what matters to the other person is innocent enough—collecting garden gnomes—then you needn't make further critical assessment if your aim is simply to be thoughtful.

Like reasonableness, thoughtfulness requires thinking about things from the point of view of another. Thoughtfulness involves recognizing others' concerns and trying to promote those concerns (where doing so is feasible, consistent with basic morality, common sense, and so on). Reasonableness requires a critical-minded assessment of the concerns of others and an open-minded readiness to change one's own concerns. In some ways thoughtfulness is more demanding than reasonableness in that you may need to suppress your critical judgment, and that might be challenging (collecting gnomes—really?). In other ways, thoughtfulness is less demanding. You can bypass the difficulties of assessing whether what matters to the other person really matters at all. If Karl were simply thoughtful, the fact of Ann's great concern would be enough to move him to stop the lesson. For this reason, sometimes thoughtfulness from others is all one wants. All Ann wants, maybe, is for Karl to give the controls back to the pilot without further involving himself in questions about whether she is right in her concerns.

Both reasonableness and thoughtfulness depend on a basic human ability to think from another person's point of view, an ability to see what matters to them. This ability is for Immanuel Kant one of the "maxims of common human understanding." Kant ([1790] 1964, 136–137) writes, "However small may be the area of degree to which a man's natural gifts reach, yet it indicates a man of enlarged thought if he disregards the subjective private conditions of his own judgment, by which so many others are confined, and reflects upon it from a universal standpoint (which he can only determine by placing himself at the standpoint of others)."

The philosopher Hannah Arendt gives us a chilling case of someone unable to think from another person's point of view. In 1961 Arendt covered the trial of Adolph Eichmann for the *New Yorker.* She later published her coverage as a book, *Eichmann in Jerusalem: A Report on the Banality of Evil.* How wrenching it must have been to sit in the audience at the trial, as Arendt did, to read the transcripts of Eichmann's interrogation, and to listen as the crimes he perpetrated were read into the record. His efficient dispatch of hundreds of thousands of Jews to their deaths in concentration camps, coupled with his calm demeanor at the trial, created a deeply unsettling experience for Arendt. She struggled to make sense of the juxtaposition of Eichmann's self-presentation and his heinous deeds. She became convinced that he did not bear malicious hatred toward the Jews, that his evil deeds sprang from something "banal." Using this term to characterize Eichmann's deeds ignited a controversy. Was Arendt apologizing for this man, lending support to the "only following orders" excuse that Eichmann tried to sell? The historian Barbara Tuchman (1982) expressed her doubts about Arendt's diagnosis: "Eichmann was an extraordinary, not an ordinary man, whose record is hardly one of the 'banality' of evil. For the author of that ineffable phrase—as applied to the murder of six million—to have been so taken in by Eichmann's version of himself as just a routine civil servant obeying orders is one of the puzzles of modern journalism."

Arendt is firm in her diagnosis. Others wanted to see Eichmann as filled with hatred for the Jews, but she believed they "missed the greatest moral and even legal challenge of the whole case" (Arendt 2006, 26). She saw something different: "The longer one listened to him, the more obvious it became . . . an inability to *think*, namely, to think from the standpoint of somebody else" (49).

Arendt's choice of words, in speaking of Eichmann's evil deeds as banal, rightly sounded alarms in her readers—"banal" is too weak for the job of describing someone who could say, "I will jump into my grave laughing, because the fact that I have the death of five million Jews on my conscience gives me extraordinary satisfaction" (46). But Arendt's diagnosis of Eichmann hits on something significant enough to help explain moral catastrophe. Her diagnosis was not that Eichmann was ordinary. It is not ordinary to be unable to think from the standpoint of somebody else. To think from the standpoint of someone else—not as a con man does, or a grifter, but as a thoughtful or reasonable person—helps one to see that what matters to others is worth recognition. A person lacking a capacity to think from others' standpoints lacks a basic human capacity that reliably grounds the moral treatment of others.

Let's return again to Karl and Ann: Is Karl unreasonable in turning their trip into an impromptu flight lesson? Someone might argue that he is being reasonable: "It is one thing to be open to the point of view of another person and another thing to anticipate the concerns of others. Maybe if Karl is thoughtful, considerate, or solicitous, he will anticipate Ann's concerns, but that's not required for him to merely be reasonable. Ann didn't speak up. So he's reasonable to take the flight lesson."

This defense of Karl's reasonableness makes it out to be a solely reactive quality. However, it is not just the thoughtful person, or the solicitous person, who anticipates the concerns of others. We also expect that a reasonable person is aware of obvious things in their environment, and aware of concerns that others have, or are likely to have, even before they are told. The law enforces these expectations: Reasonable people know relevant things about their circumstances. For instance, liability law requires people to know about hazards—the shopkeeper whose flooring is broken should know it is a tripping hazard. Not only is a reasonable person aware of obvious things, but they are also aware of things that matter. Throwing steel beams from the roof might have a lot going for it, from your point of view; it is the easiest way for you to finish up your construction job. But from the point of view of the pedestrian down below, it is a bad idea. The pedestrian's point of view should be obvious to you, up on the roof, without your having to be told. The danger to pedestrians is obvious, something one should know. Reasonableness requires being good at anticipating the typical concerns of one's fellow human beings.[1]

We can now articulate several kinds and degrees of unreasonableness. Here is a little collection of cases: First, there is not even registering a potential difference in points of view, even when it is obvious and relevant. For instance, Karl apparently hasn't begun to consider whether Ann has her own point of view on the flight lesson, despite the common knowledge that people have vastly different comfort levels in small planes. That's one degree of unreasonableness.

Then there is a degree of unreasonableness where a difference in point of view is known but a person refuses to consider it. Recall Assaf and his sister. He tells her that it is important to him to be on the same page with her, and she fails to be open to the possibility that this matters, that there is value in it. Or imagine the case of Ann and Karl happening differently: Ann pipes up and tells Karl her concerns—she manages to say, "I don't like this. If you make one small mistake, we are seconds away from hypothermia"—but Karl carries on with the lesson without considering whether her concern tracks anything that matters. This is a more extreme degree of unreasonableness.

Another degree of unreasonableness: You can fail in several ways to be appropriately critical of your own concerns or those of others. Imagine Karl listens to Ann's concern but makes an indefensible judgment about whether her concerns really matter: "My being an accomplished pilot is one of the most important things, and my opportunities to gain skills are so rare, I am willing to engage a substantial risk to my life and yours to be able to master water landings." Admittedly, this is an outlandish hypothetical. If Karl said this, we might wonder: Is he really using his judgment about the correctness of Ann's concerns? Is he really trying to get it right about what matters in this case? It sounds like he is maybe not thinking, or he is rationalizing his actions (in an unconvincing way). This would be a way of failing to be open to Ann's concerns.

Or we might imagine Karl listens to Ann's concerns and tries to be open-minded. He is not rationalizing his decision to keep flying, and is trying to get it right about what matters, but he is hopelessly bad at it. This failure would also make him unreasonable. We expect a reasonable person to be competent at tracking what matters, and to be reliable in registering value. If Karl were reasonable, he would know that his own safety and the safety of his loved one matters more than acquiring a cool skill. If he did not see that, he would be unreasonable in a distinctive way.

We are now ready to identify something fundamental to being reasonable. We have seen that if you are reasonable, you think about other people's points of view in a special way, namely, you are open to the possibility that what matters to them does in fact matter. Consequently, you are open to changes in your own point of view. But why be open-minded at all? Because, as a reasonable person, at bottom you want to get it right about value. You're open to others' concerns because you want your concerns to accurately track what really matters. You're ready to listen to others, for if something matters to another person, they might be on to something. A fundamental concern to get it right about value also explains why, if you're reasonable, you'll be critical in your assessment of what matters to others. It's not just that you're afraid of being fickle or uncritically accepting of others' viewpoints. You'll find it important to discern whether what matters to them in fact matters, because you're concerned to accurately track what really matters.

Now someone might worry that this account of reasonableness makes it seem highly individualistic. We want to explain the prosocial side of a reasonable person. "You say being reasonable involves being concerned to get it right about value—where's the sociality in that?" The answer is that if you are concerned to correctly identify what matters, that explains why you engage in socially minded decision-making; it explains why you recognize the needs and interests of others and are willing to modify your own goals. Recall the landowner who controls most of the water in his county. If he is reasonable, he is concerned to track what matters in his situation. Consequently, he is open to the possibility that what matters to his neighbors (getting a minimal supply of water) is something that in fact matters. In this case, it is obvious that it does matter a great deal since water is essential for life. It does not take much critical intelligence for the landowner to see that what matters to his neighbors actually matters. He may weigh his concerns against theirs: It matters to him to maximize his crop yield, and it matters to them to survive. When he weighs these things, he quickly sees what matters more. The concern to accurately track value will make a person sensitive to the concerns of others and ready to modify their own concerns where conflict arises, if doing so promotes the things that matter most.

One might also wonder whether saying *a reasonable person is concerned to get it right about value* suggests that a reasonable person only cares about what matters to others in an instrumental way, using others as one might use an instrument, like a Geiger counter, to detect value. Is that right? No—the Geiger counter picture distorts a reasonable person's fundamental concern with understanding what is of value and promoting it. Of course, sometimes another person has information about what is of value, and a reasonable person will use this information if they have it. Why wouldn't they? But a reasonable person is not a selfish collector of information about what matters, hoarding knowledge about where value lies. A reasonable person is cooperative, interested in sharing their understanding of what really matters. Why? Because a reasonable person can see it matters that everyone forms accurate judgments about what is of value and what is not. Moreover, a reasonable person does not just learn what matters to others as a way of finding out about value. They learn about what matters to others for all sorts of reasons, for all the kinds of value that this understanding can promote. For example, friendship only exists between people who care to understand what matters to their friends. Friendship and other important sorts of relationships would not be possible if one did not value understanding what matters to others.

Are we to imagine that, in an easy case like the landowner's, or Karl's flight lesson, if one is reasonable, one will find a change in one's own point of view quick and effortless? No. Being reasonable is not always easy for us. A reasonable person does not necessarily find their emotions, desires, and goals instantly falling into line with what they judge to matter most. Given the strength of the landowner's desire to maximize his own crop, or Karl's desire to master a new piloting skill, and given their emotional investments in their goals, it might take a lot of effort to come around to their newfound point of view.

A good question to ask is how one manages to be reasonable. Being reasonable involves being concerned to get it right about what matters. This can be difficult. It requires being both open-minded and critically minded, which can be taxing. Being reasonable is work. If you are concerned to get it right about what really has value, you must wade into the messy business of evaluating what matters to yourself and to others. How do we do all this? It can sound like you need to escape your own point of view to critically assess what really matters. If I were saying that a reasonable person must somehow occupy a godlike perspective on which things have value and which don't, that would be crazy. It must be humanly possible to be reasonable.

Let's investigate how mere humans manage to be reasonable.

4

Mapping the Landscape of Value

Rudy Stanko—driving eighty-five miles per hour on a two-lane highway with frost heaves and curves, with no way to stop had a farmer been crossing the road—violated Montana's requirement to drive reasonably. Driving reasonably takes thought about what is important, not just to oneself but to others too. Stanko did a bad job of that, however skillfully he handled his car. Someone might object: How exactly is Stanko supposed to think about what is important to others? Is he supposed to somehow escape his own point of view on what matters, to achieve a godlike view of what is important? That sounds impossible.

Stanko could be reasonable without having to make a superhuman escape from his own point of view. To see how, let's develop an understanding of how one manages to think about what matters. We can start by exploring the difference between what matters to you and what matters, period.

What goes on when something matters to you? The Covid-19 pandemic changed what mattered to many of us. In August 2022, with newly lifted restrictions on public life, the Pew Research Center investigated how Americans felt their priorities had changed (Sharpe and Spencer 2022). Many people (26 percent) said that keeping healthy became newly important to them—not just avoiding the virus, but also "staying healthy, exercising, eating right and watching out for my mental health." And 10 percent of those polled found that work did not matter as much. As one person said, "When I worked from home, I was able to be very efficient and finish work during my contract hours. Now that I am back to commuting and interacting with colleagues, that is more difficult to do, but I do not take home work-tasks any longer. My family time is too valuable."

Sam Scheffler, a philosopher, dissects what goes on in you when something matters to you. He identifies four elements. First, there's an emotional element. Scheffler uses his own case of his relationship with his brother to illustrate:

> If my relationship with my brother matters to me, then I may feel pleased at the prospect of spending time with him, saddened if we rarely have occasion to see one another, eager to help him if he is in need, distressed if a serious conflict develops between us or if we become estranged, and shocked and betrayed if he harms me or abuses my trust. (Scheffler 2011, 28)

If something matters to you, you are susceptible to various emotions. Just which emotions you'll be susceptible to depends on the thing that matters to you. Scheffler notes that if his brother's character were problematic, their relationship would be different, and then, he notes, "I would not actually be shocked—only disappointed and resigned—if he abused my trust" (28). If you are not susceptible to *any* emotions about a thing, then it is not correct to say that the thing matters to you. If Sam truly does not feel anything one way or another about spending time with his brother, then his relationship with his brother does not matter to him.

Emotional susceptibility can be hard to detect, so an observer can find it hard to know what matters to you. Sam's relationship to his brother might matter a lot to him, but if the relationship kindles painful emotions, he might work to suppress or deny his feelings.

His outward behavior might have observers thinking the relationship does not matter to him, even though it matters a lot.

A second element in something's mattering to you is believing the thing matters, period. What does it mean for a thing to matter, period? This is one of the larger questions humans face, but Scheffler's answer is refreshingly brief: The thing needs to be valuable, worthy, or good in some way. A brotherly relationship is a valuable thing. Valuable things have features that give their value a specific character. Sam's relationship with his brother matters—it is valuable—and it has various features Sam is sensitive to in valuing it.[1] The relationship is *a source of sustenance* to them, and *it gives them joy*. Because of these features, Sam has particular reasons to value his relationship with his brother. Imagine Sam lacks the belief that his relationship is valuable—or just to make the point vivid, imagine he believes the opposite: he thinks, "My relationship with my brother is a dead loss. It's more like a relationship with a stranger, no closeness, no joy." If this were so, it would be mystifying if Sam insisted that the relationship nonetheless matters to him. To dispel the mystery, we might go for an alternative explanation, saying that Sam hopes for a brotherly relationship, and he is emotionally engaged by this possibility; what matters to him is the relationship he could maybe have someday, not the relationship he currently has.

You might ask, must one really believe a thing is valuable for it to matter to one? "Can't the watch my grandfather bequeathed matter to me, even though I also believe that it is not valuable?" No. In that case, it has some sort of value that is not monetary. It is not the case that utterly valueless things can matter to you, but rather there are many ways a thing can be valuable. You might know the watch has no monetary value, yet if the watch matters to you, then you believe it has some value—perhaps it's an heirloom with historical value, or it has sentimental value. If it matters to you, you'll think the watch has some sort of value or worth. Scheffler's point is that you cannot value something, or have it matter to you, while also believing the thing really does not matter at all. For instance, say it matters to you to have ice cream in the freezer, on hand for when you want some. Can you at the same time think it does not matter to have ice cream in the freezer? No. It might not matter much, and it might not matter to others. But you think having ice cream on hand is a good thing. Were you to believe having ice cream on hand is of absolutely no value or worth, then it wouldn't matter to you.

A third element: When something matters to you, you experience your emotions about the thing as making sense. If Sam feels distress when a conflict develops between him and his brother, his distress makes sense to him: Something he believes to be valuable is threatened. If your grandfather's watch matters to you, then if you lose it, your frustration and sadness at the loss make sense to you. Imagine someone were to challenge you: "Why are you so upset? It was hardly an expensive watch." You could explain yourself: "It has great sentimental value."

A fourth element, Scheffler says, is that if something matters to you, it will affect your thinking about what you have reason to do. Spending time with my son matters a lot to me. That gives me reason to change my schedule when he's free. If I never see any reason to change my schedule to make time for my son, it would not be correct to say that spending time with him matters to me. If something matters to you, it shapes your reasons about how to act.

These basic elements—emotional engagement, belief in the thing's value, experiencing your emotions as sensible, and reasoning about how to act—are welded to each other. Reasons are what weld them together. Sam's belief about the value of his relationship with his brother is based on reasons rooted in positive features of the relationship; his emotions and his actions are sensitive to these same reasons. The value of his relationship makes sensible both his distress over conflicts and his taking action to keep the relationship strong.

We have been discussing cases of positive value, but the value of a thing might be negative. If Sam notices a rattlesnake on the hiking trail ahead of him, he believes that it matters to avoid the snake. He believes a close encounter with the snake would be of great disvalue. In believing this, he is justified in his beliefs about what matters in the situation he is in. Being justified in one's beliefs means having good evidence or reasons, and Sam has good reason to avoid rattlesnakes.

Scheffler's observations help us grasp the difference between what matters to you and what matters, period. If something matters to a person, they feel emotionally invested in the thing, because they believe it valuable, for reasons that make sense of their valuing it. If something matters period, by contrast, the thing just is valuable, worthy, or good in some way.

Being a reasonable person does not require superhuman feats, or an impossible transcendence of one's own point of view. A reasonable person is concerned to get it right about what matters—about what is valuable, worthy, or good. Having this concern, a reasonable person will tend to seek reasons, or evidence, or justification for their beliefs about what matters.[2] Suppose Sam is a reasonable person and suppose his relationship with his brother matters to him. He feels emotionally invested in it because he believes that the relationship is valuable, and he has good reasons for thinking so. Being reasonable, Sam wants to have good reasons for his belief that his relationship is valuable. This is not to say that he must consciously reflect on, or be very articulate about, his reasons. Sensitivity to reasons can be inarticulate.

Imagine that Sam's brother is scamming him, seeking Sam's financial support, and only pretending to enjoy his time with Sam. If Sam finds out about the fraud, he no longer has good reason to believe that his relationship with his brother is valuable. If he's reasonable, this will make an immediate difference to him. He is concerned to get it right about what is valuable, and given the damning evidence, he will no longer be able to see the relationship as valuable. If Sam is tempted to ignore the evidence of his brother's fraud, that might be understandable—his desire for a brotherly relationship might be strong—but ignoring the evidence would make him unreasonable. If Sam retains hope and seeks to change his brother by showing him what boundless faith in a person looks like, that might be a reasonable goal, so long as Sam is open-eyed, and he doesn't ignore the evidence that his relationship is, in its current form, without value.

You do not have to escape your own point of view to be reasonable. You do not have to stop having the things that matter to you matter to you or abandon your own concerns. You do need to be concerned to get it right about what matters in the situation you are in. That means being sensitive to whether your beliefs about what matters are justified beliefs. Sometimes the reasons stack up against your point of view. When they do, painful as it may be, you must admit you are wrong about what is of value.

Not everything you believe to be valuable can matter to you. When something—a relationship, a memento—matters to you, you are emotionally vulnerable to its welfare. If it fares badly, you will feel bad, and if it fares well, you will be pleased. But, as Scheffler explains, "most people have a capacity for the recognition of value that far outstrips their capacity for emotional vulnerability" (2011, 31). Humans have only so much emotional capacity, and only so many things can engage your emotions in the way required for them to matter to you. Fortunately, our limited emotional bandwidth does not prevent us from seeing that there is value in things we are not personally engaged with. You can believe things to be valuable, or worthy, or good, even though they do not matter to you personally. Sam's relationship with his brother matters to him, but it does not matter to you. You do not feel emotionally invested in their relationship or emotionally vulnerable to its ups and downs. Still, the value of Sam's relationship is something that you can understand. If you have trouble understanding it, he can explain to you why he believes it is valuable. ("We're always there for each other.") So, even if their relationship does not matter to you personally, as a reasonable person you can believe it matters, for the same reasons Sam does. Despite the diversity of things that matter to each of us, we find grounds for mutual comprehension in our justified beliefs about what is valuable. Reasonable people are sensitive to such grounds.

To be reasonable, you are concerned to get it right about what matters, and you reliably track things that matter, but you do not have to be omniscient about value. Neither do you need to be infallible in your beliefs: Reasonable people can make mistakes about what matters.

Let me say a bit more about mistakes. Being reasonable does not require infallibility. It does not mean being perfectly correct all the time about what matters. If you are reasonable, you are invested in forming justified beliefs about what is valuable. You won't always succeed in having true beliefs about what is valuable. Your justified beliefs can be false.

To illustrate the point, imagine you have a justified belief about the sentimental value of a watch in your possession: You have memories of your grandfather giving you his watch and of his telling you he wanted you to have a memento from him. Now suppose that the watch in your possession is not your grandfather's. That watch was lost when you were little, and your grandmother, knowing how much it meant to you, replaced it with an exact duplicate. Imagine she goes to her grave having kept a perfect secret—there is no trace of evidence to suggest you are wrong about the value of the watch. Your belief that the watch in your possession has great sentimental value is false, but you have good reason to believe what you do—you remember his giving you a watch and you justifiably take it to be this one. So, although you are wrong about its value, it is reasonable for you to value the watch. It is reasonable for you to believe it has value.

What about a case where someone lacks any good reason to believe a thing is valuable? Recall our outlandish example of Warren, who turns on every radio he sees whenever he can. There is no good reason for thinking this is a valuable activity. If Warren says, "it's a worthy pursuit" we might credit him with making an effort—we might say, "he's trying to be reasonable." But his failure to get it right about what matters is so spectacular, we cannot say he is reasonable in what he does. Being reasonable does not require being right all the time about what matters, but it does require having good reasons for one's beliefs about what matters.[3] One's reasons do not have to be so strong that they would survive all criticism or further discoveries.[4] Say that in the future you will find evidence of your grandmother's scheme to replace the watch—so your *justification* for believing the watch valuable is *defeasible*. Nonetheless you have good reason to think the watch valuable, so you are reasonable in valuing it.

Our idea of a reasonable person does not require infallibility, but it does involve being good at tracking both positive and negative value. In addition to getting it right about obvious things that matter, a reasonable person will have good reasons for their beliefs about what is valuable.

One might be inclined to say about cases of error, "Well, but what matters to you just matters to you, and even if you are mistaken in your belief that the thing is valuable, or what its value is, it still matters to you." That's all true. The point is that even though you mistake the thing's value, you can have a justified belief that it is valuable. And having a justified belief is what it takes to be reasonable in valuing it. We should also acknowledge that good things can come from mistakes. Treasuring what one mistakenly takes to be valuable might do one a great deal of good. The treasuring of the watch can matter, even if the watch is no treasure.

Discovering your mistakes about what matters can be painful. The possibility of errors can lead some people to a nihilistic fear that nothing really matters: "I used to think it mattered what strangers thought of my fashion choices, but I was wrong . . . maybe in the future whatever I think matters now will seem wrong, too. . . . Maybe nothing matters!" The best response to this nihilistic worry is to remember that where you can get it wrong, you can also get it right. We may have to struggle to learn about things that matter, and we may make mistakes along the way, but making errors about what matters does not mean that nothing matters.

Some people are committed nihilists about value. They think nothing matters and that it is wrong to believe that anything is valuable, worthy, or good. This thought is sometimes said to arise if we consider "the standpoint of eternity," from which supposedly we can see that nothing really matters. My own view is that nihilism about value is a mistake—especially if it supposedly arises from the "standpoint of eternity." Thomas Nagel (1971) suggests that the viewpoint of eternity leads to a "way of perceiving our true situation." But a viewpoint from which nothing matters misses some important things. At least as good a candidate for being my true situation is the one revealed by my viewpoint. That said, if nihilism about value is true and nothing whatsoever matters, there are still reasonable people. Reasonable people are concerned to get it right about what matters, and they strive to have justified beliefs about what is valuable; if nihilism is true, they have a lot of false beliefs—they are mistaken about things having value—but they have plenty of good reason to think these things have value. You have plenty of reason to think that, to paraphrase a Lucinda Williams song (1988), a comfortable bed that won't hurt your back, food to fill you up, and warm clothes, and all that stuff are valuable.

So far, we've been exploring what it takes to be a reasonable person: it requires a concern to form justified beliefs about what matters. But that is not all it takes. Life's decisions force us to figure out which things matter more than others, among all the things that matter in a situation. Sometimes it is easy to know which things matter more than others. In 1988 Ed Webster was part of a small team that climbed to the top of Mount Everest, making the first ascent of a new route on its remote east face without oxygen, radios, or Sherpa assistance. To hear him describe his adventure, what mattered to Webster wasn't the headline-grabbing nature of the feat, but simply being on Everest. As much as it mattered to him, he turned back three hundred feet shy of the summit. His decision, made between bouts of blacking out from hypoxia, was simple: "I knew I would die if I tried to go on," he said.

Many times, it is not so easy to know which things matter more than others. Consequently, making decisions can be difficult. Benjamin Franklin suggested a method. List the pros and cons of a particular course of action, weighting them by how much they matter, and then strike off equal items from each side: "Thus proceeding I find at length where the Ballance lies; and if after a Day or two of farther Consideration nothing new that is of Importance occurs on either side, I come to a Determination accordingly" ([1772] 1976, 299–300). Franklin's tool preceded modern decision theory by more than a century. Today, theorists model rational decision-making by assigning numeric values to the outcomes of possible courses of action. Take the raincoat or leave it at home? Carrying it if there is no rain is a cost, but if it rains there is a benefit. The answer about what to do is: Take the course of action with the greatest expected utility, given the probability of rain. Turning our decisions about what to do into questions about how to maximize expected utility is wonderfully useful.[5] But calculating expected utilities in no way removes the need to reflect on which things matter more than others: How important is staying dry in the rain? How much do you disvalue lugging around your raincoat on a sunny day? Utility calculations—in Franklin's rustic form or in modern decision-theoretic dress—require us to assign values to outcomes, and assigning values just returns us to the problem of judging which things matter more than others.

The task gets tougher in cases where the things that matter are incommensurable—that is, where there is no common scale we can use to weigh things against each other. In fact, if the philosopher Joseph Raz is right, the task gets impossible. Raz gives an example. Carla is a talented person, and she has a choice between two careers:

one as a lawyer and one as a musician. She will be a success in whichever she chooses. Neither career seems better than the other. Both careers are attractive, in different ways. Her two options hold such different attractions, though, that she cannot say they are equally good. If they were equally good, Raz argues, then if Carla could make her legal career even slightly better, say, by the addition of a bit more excitement or money, that would break the tie, and her choice would be clear. But her choice is not clear. Carla still finds the choice between music and lawyering difficult, even with the added money or excitement. Each option still pulls on her (Raz 1988, 332).

Maybe in some situations, one thing comes to matter so much that competing things just stop mattering all together. Moral philosopher Elizabeth Anderson gives us a case:

> Consider the captain of a sinking ship, who must coordinate the efforts of the crew to get people into lifeboats. It could be a fact about this captain that slipping off to his quarters to catch a nip of sherry would be a great relief and pleasure for him in these stressful hours. (Anderson 1995, 37)

If he's reasonable, the captain does not retreat to his cabin but immediately turns to evacuating his passengers. Why? Here's one view: The captain believes that a quiet drink in his cabin has value, but he also realizes that saving his passengers has greater value, and seeing what matters more, he responds appropriately, starting the evacuation. Here is another view: In the situation at hand, having a drink in his cabin has no value whatsoever. Anderson explains: "If the captain is virtuous, this fact will not even enter his mind as a potentially relevant consideration bearing upon what he should do now. The consideration is 'silenced'" (37). In the circumstances, the captain believes that slipping away to his cabin does not matter at all. Evacuating his passengers is the only thing that matters in the situation at hand. Deep questions about the nature of value need answers before we can choose between these competing accounts of the case.[6] Is there something valuable—something that matters, just a little bit—that the captain must forfeit to do his duty? Or does what matters depend on the circumstances, and there is nothing even a little bit valuable that the captain sacrifices?

Life would be easier if our circumstances sorted out for us what matters. Maybe this happens sometimes, and the truest description of our choice is that it was no choice at all. But many times, difficult choices involve a tug of war between competing things that clearly matter.

Our idea of a reasonable person involves the idea of being good at knowing which things matter more than others. Turning back from a deadly summit attempt, saving the passengers on a sinking boat—these are the easy cases. Life throws us much trickier cases. How do we grapple with them?

Admittedly there is no algorithm, no simple rule to follow that tells us which things matter more than others. We bring a wide array of competences to questions of comparative value each time we face them. It takes experience and hard work to acquire the capacity to judge the relative merits when values compete. Jay Wallace, moral theorist, calls our capacity for practical deliberation a capacity for "mapping the landscape of value."[7] This metaphor aptly sums up what we expect of ourselves as reasonable people: We are good at mapping the landscape of value. As we form justified beliefs about what matters more than what, we are charting the mountains and the molehills of the value landscape. There is no simple rule for weighing competing values against each other, but we do manage to do it. If there are incommensurable values and if we're reasonable, we are sensitive to the impossibility of a simple weighing procedure to settle the question. We recognize there are hard cases.

Someone might object here about the very idea of being concerned to get it right about value. We disagree about lots and there can be big cultural and personal differences in what matters to us. Pain is bad, sure. Getting basic needs met is good, sure. But we disagree about lots of other values. So someone might object, what can it even mean to say a reasonable person is concerned to map the value landscape?

Let's clarify the objection. We might put the worry in terms of *relativism* about value—the idea that what is of value or disvalue depends on one's perspective or one's culture. We can distinguish relativism about value from the idea that value is *relational.* Relationalism about value is the idea that the evolution of sentient beings who could feel pain and who had interests (for example, an interest in living, in procreating, in being free of pain) is necessary for value and disvalue to exist. Relationalism is consistent with the idea that some things, such as pain, pleasure, and satisfying basic needs for food, shelter, human companionship, have a claim to being universal values. Suppose that some values are not just relational in their nature but also exist only relative to a culture. Being cool, let's suppose, is not something people universally value, and in some cultures, it might have no value. In a culture where no one values being cool, relativism implies no one is making a mistake. The question is, if all value depends on culture, how would you defend the account of being reasonable as being concerned to get it right about value?

Here's one response. If all value is culturally relative, then the value a reasonable person is concerned to track will vary from culture to culture. We might say, "Ed Webster is reasonable," and mean that Ed is good at mapping the values his culture makes possible. Alternatively, we might say "Ed is reasonable" in a more capacious way, to say that Ed has a capacity to track different values across various cultures, that he is concerned to get it right about more things than just the values his culture makes possible. We might need to clarify which application of "reasonable" we have in mind. Either way, the notion of an adept value-mapper would have an important use, even under the supposition of total cultural relativism.

Humans are social creatures. So far, we have explored how ordinary people manage to be reasonable—how they manage to think about what matters—but we have not explored how ordinary people think *together* about what matters. Reasonable people are concerned to do so. Reasonable people seek to create shareable maps of value.[8] That is to say, they share with each other their beliefs about what is valuable, with the goal of helping each other track what's of value. There is value in sharing our beliefs about what's valuable, and a reasonable person appreciates this value, too. But agreement in our beliefs about value can prove difficult to come by. Getting our value maps to align can be tricky. It can be a challenge even to know about another person's viewpoint. Cultural difference, generational difference, personal idiosyncrasy, and a host of other barriers can obstruct one's knowledge of what others value. Recently, I had a student in my class who is a member of the Lakota tribe. She learned as a child that it was disrespectful to make eye contact with elders and teachers, so when she spoke to me, she was always careful to cast her eyes down. I believed she was shy, and I wanted her to feel free to look me in the eye. I did not realize she was acting in accord with what mattered to her. As it happened, we agreed on something that matters—showing respect is a good thing—but I did not know that this concern was behind her behavior.

It can also be a challenge, once one knows about another's viewpoint, to see reasons for it. Some people see no reason to think climbing Everest a worthy goal. From their point of view—the "Why-would-anyone-do-such-a-thing?" point of view—Ed Webster's story holds little interest, except maybe for what it reveals about the psychological pushes and pulls of extreme behavior. Psychologist Frank Farley identifies a "Type T" personality as the psychological cause of thrill-seeking behavior. Farley reckons as many as one third of Americans are Type T personalities: "They want an exciting, interesting and thrilling life," says Farley. "At the end of their lives, they want to say they lived it" (Rouvalis 2006). If one is unable to see

Webster's reasons for mountain climbing, one can revert to Farley's psychological explanation. Farley says, "You can look at these people and say, 'They are stupid.' But I might say, 'That is their personality.'" It may seem more respectful of Webster to say that he has a Type T personality than to say that he is stupid. But an explanation of his mountain climbing in terms of his personality type does not even try to engage his point of view. It is an explanation that takes no note of what he believes valuable and why. At least when you call Webster stupid, you are crediting him with beliefs about what matters and reasons for his beliefs—reasons you judge to be bad, but reasons nonetheless.

If we could only ever understand each other by diagnosing the causes of each other's behavior—"You're a Type T, a Virgo, born in the year of the Rabbit"—our own lives would be poorer. Engaging with others over what matters to them and why can make us more flexible in our own valuing and help us find value where we would not if left to our own devices. To hear Webster talk about it, Everest presented an extraordinary challenge to him as a modestly gifted climber, and the long and patient effort just to undertake the adventure gave unity and organization to his life. Understanding his reasons might give you a new perspective on extreme challenges. If you are reasonable, and you really listen and understand his reasons for valuing what he does, it might change your point of view.

Most of us readily agree about some major landmarks on the map of value. Ed Webster's choosing life over death on Everest is an instance of getting it right about value. Karl and Ann have different points of view on the flight lesson—different things matter to them about it; nonetheless with discussion and sharing reasons for their beliefs, they may achieve a meeting of minds about the value of safety. But even when it comes to major landmarks, we do not always agree about which things have greater value than others, or even whether they have value at all. This gives rise to a different kind of worry about my account of reasonableness. Given our individual differences, how can we hope to build shareable maps of the value landscape?

We can start by distinguishing various kinds of disagreement. Some points of view are too alien for us to make sense of. Warren, who turns on every radio he sees, has a point of view on what matters that is perplexing to us, and we cannot see a way to overlay his map of value on our own. The problem resolves if we stop trying to see Warren as in the business of valuing things, but rather in the grip of an obsession. Then our disagreement can be chalked up to pathology and it does not threaten the very idea of sharing a map of value with others.

What about disagreement among mutually intelligible people? Some differences in what matters to people owe merely to differences in emotional engagement. Imagine this case: it matters a lot to your friend to attend church, and it does not matter to you. You lack the emotional engagement with churchgoing that your friend experiences. In this case, your disagreement does not necessarily create a barrier to building a shared value map. Different things matter to different people, and given the limits of our emotional bandwidth, we can expect differences in what matters to you and your friend. You could nonetheless both agree in the belief that churchgoing is valuable. You could mark this as a point on a shared map of the value landscape.

Our disagreements sometimes go deeper. Change the case: Imagine that you believe church attendance is not valuable. You acknowledge it may produce some valuable things. You see that it lifts your friend's spirits, gives him solace, and makes him more patient. If churchgoing made your friend downcast and impatient, however, you would see no reason at all for him to attend. Your friend sees attendance as valuable—a worthy or good thing, regardless of what further goods it produces. Your friend sees churchgoing as intrinsically valuable. You see churchgoing as having instrumental value at best—it produces for your friend some downstream consequences that are themselves intrinsically valuable. The prospects of your agreeing about how to map value—at least in this corner of the value terrain—are dim. You would mark the positive downstream effects of churchgoing on a map of value, but not churchgoing itself. Your friend draws the map differently.

Doesn't the fact of this sort of deep disagreement lead to doubt about the goal of sharing judgments about value? We have seen that a reasonable person is concerned to get it right about what matters—about value and disvalue. If what matters looks quite different to different people, then doesn't that mean there is no such thing as creating a shared map of the value landscape?

In cases of thinner disagreement—Rudy Stanko's, Menlove's—people are just getting it wrong about value. Menlove and Stanko are wrong about the danger their actions produced. The fact of their disagreement with others in no way threatens the idea that there is such a thing as sharing judgments of value. In the churchgoing case, however, value looks quite different to different people, and it might seem no one is getting value wrong. This looks like a deep disagreement. Maybe there is no single right answer about the value of churchgoing. So, one might ask, what sense is there to talking about being concerned to share a judgment about the answer?

In response, here is the key point: If there is no single right answer about the value of churchgoing, then a person who is concerned to get it right about value will be concerned to acknowledge this fact. A reasonable person will be concerned to distinguish the various kinds of disagreement we have just outlined. And where deep disagreement exists, a reasonable person will be concerned to acknowledge it. Where there is no single right answer about what matters, a reasonable person will be concerned to note as much. That's the lay of the land—it's how the landscape of value lies. So, deep disagreement does not threaten the very idea of seeking to share value judgments. When the value landscape is complex and contested, if you are a reasonable person you absolutely want to acknowledge as much. Face to face with deep disagreement about value, reasonable people do not pretend things are simple.

An objector might press, "What good is being reasonable, if we don't agree on what has value?" I think that is the wrong question. Reasonable people will be concerned when others disagree. They will want to understand the nature of the disagreement. Am I making a mistake, or is the other guy? Are we both making a mistake? Is there no such thing as getting it right in this case? These are the kinds of question a reasonable person will ask in the face of disagreement. They are good questions to ask. Maybe if the value landscape were more easily navigated, we would have no use for the idea of a person who can navigate it well.

How can we create sharable maps of value? We disagree about lots, and there can be big cultural differences in what matters to us. But humans are social creatures, and we want to share our beliefs about what is valuable, worthy and good. How can we do it?

5

Disagreement and Sharing Maps of Value

Humans are evaluators. From the moment we wake up, we register value and disvalue in our environment. A reasonable person is concerned to get it right about value, which is often a shared endeavor. Acting together, we help each other discover things to pursue and to avoid in our environment. We also disagree about value all the time. We have discrepant impressions of what's good, worthy, tasty, scary, and so on. How then can we jointly map the value landscape?

Take disagreement about aesthetic value or matters of taste. Common proverbs enforce a theme: We should not expect agreement in matters of taste. Whether it's about the yumminess of cherry pie, the pleasant "roundness" of umami, or the savoriness of aquavit, people say: "To each his own," "One man's meat is another man's poison," "There's no accounting for taste." People also often say that there is no point in arguing about taste. This sentiment goes at least as far back as the Latin proverb "De gustibus non est disputandum" ("As for taste, it should not be disputed"). Proverbial wisdom has it that beauty, unlike *being made of carbon*, say, or *being square,* is in the eye of the beholder. It seems an easy step to the idea that we should not bother trying to share our judgments about aesthetic value.

The famous Scottish philosopher David Hume (1711–1776) thinks the proverbial wisdom is mistaken. He asks us to reflect on our practices. Think about how we would react to someone who makes crazy comparative judgments. Who would say Sid Vicious is a better bassist than John Entwistle?[1] "There may be found" persons ready to make outrageous judgments, Hume notes, but "no one pays attention to such a taste; and we pronounce, without scruple, the sentiment of these pretended critics to be absurd and ridiculous." Our dismissive reaction to "Vicious is better than Entwistle" shows that we don't think taste is entirely subjective after all. We think sometimes a person can just get it wrong in their aesthetic value judgments.

On Hume's view, our judgments of taste track those things that give us pleasure. Over time, our judgments tend to converge on "beauties" that are "naturally fitted to excite agreeable sentiments" when appropriately attended to. (The winged Assyrian lamassu guarding the citadel of Sargon II have stood the test of time.) And according to Hume, there is a standard that settles questions about aesthetic value. Hume repeats this story from Miguel de Cervantes's novel *Don Quixote*. Sancho tells the Don that he is descended from a long line of excellent judges of wine:

> Two of my kinsmen were once called to give their opinion of a hogshead, which was supposed to be excellent, being old and of a good vintage. One of them tastes it; considers it; and, after mature reflection, pronounces the wine to be good, were it not for a small taste of leather, which he perceived in it. The other, after using the same precautions, gives also his verdict in favour of the wine; but with the reserve of a taste of iron, which he could easily distinguish. You cannot imagine how much they were both ridiculed for their judgment. But who laughed in the end? On emptying the hogshead, there was found at the bottom an old key with a leathern thong tied to it. (1987, 235)

Hume uses this story to suggest there can be proof that one is tracking things accurately with one's judgment of taste. When the wine barrel was emptied and the key was found at the bottom, this proved the tasters correct in their judgment of the wine.

Hume is joking a bit with this story. He knows that proving a person is right in a judgment of taste is not so simple as finding a key in a wine barrel. His point is that we recognize that we can refine our taste, and so there is something to the idea of a standard of correctness for our judgments of taste. Imagine a person who works hard to cultivate his taste. He buys the sommelier smell kit and trains himself to recognize the aromas in red wine. When he makes a judgment about the tastiness of a wine, his judgment depends on a heightened sensitivity to the wine's features—its acids, sugars, alcohol, and phenolic compounds. Imagine our wine aficionado not only refines his sensitivity to these features, but he also gains wide experience and works to free his mind of prejudice (not letting his cultural prejudice sway his judgment). Now, put a group of such people together—people who combine sensitivity, experience, and an absence of bias. Agreement among them, according to Hume, is the standard or proof of correct aesthetic judgment:

> Strong sense, united to delicate sentiment, improved by practice, perfected by comparison, and cleared of all prejudice, can alone entitle critics to this valuable character. The joint verdict of such, wherever they are to be found, is the true standard of taste and beauty. (1987, 241)

So, according to Hume, we have a way of deciding who is right about the tastiness of the wine. It is whoever would be judged correct by such a panel of judges.

Hume might be wrong about a lot. He might be wrong that our taste judgments track items that give us pleasure, and wrong that there is a standard of correctness for taste judgments to be found in a panel of trained judges. He is right about a couple of things, though. There is commonsense behind the idea of being a better or worse judge of value, and in many cases, a good judge fits Hume's description. If you were to try to improve the reliability of your taste judgments, you would want to follow Hume's suggestions: You'd want to practice, compare your judgments with those of others, and work to free yourself from prejudice. (You would also do well to remember that these qualities cannot do the whole job of improving your performance as a judge of taste: Aesthetic judgment requires "strong sense," which is a feature of your body. If as a lifelong smoker your taste buds are not as sensitive anymore, then you cannot compensate for the loss.)

Hume is also right that, if we just look at how we behave, we don't seem to buy the proverbs. Just think about how often we encourage others to give things a whirl. "You've got to listen to this new album," "Try a taste, you'll love it." If we meet resistance from our audience, we do not always fall back on "Well, I like it." Sometimes we push: We point out specific features of the things we like, and we urge others to appreciate them: "Listen to the way the motif returns," "The caraway is a perfect complement to the onion."

Our actions speak louder than our proverbs.[2] In practice, the way we talk about aesthetic value shows that we do not take ourselves to merely be expressing individual preferences. When you say, "This movie is great," you are not saying, "I like this movie." If that were all anyone was ever saying—"I like it"—there would be no disputing about taste. You would be saying you like it, and I would be saying I didn't, and that would be the end of the discussion. But that is not always the only thing that we are saying. When you tell me the movie is great, you are going out on a limb, making a flat-out assertion about the value of the movie. And you are applying a bit of pressure. There is in your remark what philosophers call *normative force.*[3] You are suggesting that I would get something out of the movie, and that if I am judging correctly, I will also find it great.

When you tell me the movie is great, you are sending what theorists call a "costly signal." It takes you significant epistemic work to make this claim and to defend it if you're challenged. By "epistemic work" I mean you need evidence for your claim, and you need to be ready to defend it with reasons; you have to know something about the movie to make the claim. You could say instead, "Well, I liked it." This would be a cheap signal. Cheap in the sense that the epistemic cost to you of saying you like it is small: To make this remark, all you need is sincere self-knowledge. Likewise, to defend this remark costs you little. If someone challenges you over your saying, "I liked it," your reply can simply be to shrug and repeat yourself.[4] The receiver of your cheap signal, your audience, does not learn much of direct relevance to herself. Hearing your remark, I might think, "How nice for you, you found a movie you like." I am left with work to do if I am to decide what your remark means for me. When you send a costly signal—saying "It's wonderful!"—the epistemic expense for you is greater; you are going out on a limb, and you need some reason to think others will find value in the movie. To defend this claim, you need to do more than re-express your feeling; you might get challenged or asked for details or reasons. The benefit to me of your sending a costly signal is correspondingly greater. You give me an assurance that I will find value in the movie.

Why do we send and receive costly signals? Why not just stick to cheaper claims? One simple answer: because we benefit from a practice of exchanging information about value. You are helping me find something in the world that is of value, something that I would find appealing, funny, uplifting, or the like. With your costly signal you apply a bit of normative pressure—you encourage me to give the movie a chance. Even if my initial reaction is cool, your costly signal prods me to pay attention, putting me on the lookout for value I might otherwise have missed.

We expect others to share their judgments of value. It would be a drag to be around someone who only ever said, "Don't take it from me, I just like this movie." We want others to make the leap and say it's good. We want others' guidance; we want the benefit of their point of view and their sensitivity to the world's value. On the sending side, we want to share our impressions of value. Helping others find things of value is one of life's satisfactions.

We humans share lots of things—food, tools, and information. Another thing we share is our judgments about value. Even in matters of taste—an area where we can disagree starkly—the idea of sharing judgments about value makes sense. We send and receive costly signals because of the benefits of doing so, and we do it all the time.

Reasonableness has a major role in making it possible to send costly signals about value. To understand this role, it helps to attend to the many things we each must do, to keep up a healthy practice of sharing value judgments:

(i) We each must discipline our claims about value so that they do not answer only to our personal preferences, or individual impressions. Imagine Vizzini says, "I said it was a fantastic movie. I liked it, and that settles it—that is what it means to be 'fantastic.'" Not only is his utterance a cheap signal, he makes the mistake of supposing that something cheap is all that we mean by the word. But that's not so: when he says it is a fantastic movie, he is committed to its being a movie that others can use their aesthetic judgment to find value in, too.[5]

(ii) We need to accept the responsibility that comes with sending costly signals: for instance, suppose Vizzini says it's a fantastic movie, and on the strength of his remark, you go to see it. The movie is wretchedly bad. When asked "Why did you think that was a fantastic movie?" Vizzini shrugs, "I don't know." He doesn't stand behind his claim at all. This isn't how our practice works. When standing behind a claim, it is ideal if we are ready to articulate reasons for our judgment. If we cannot articulate fully explicit reasons, we can give a pointer to the qualities that we believe confer value on the movie ("the characters, the special effects"). If we cannot do even this much, we can at least tell others why our judgment might be worth their time: "I've seen a million action flicks, I have a lot of experience."

(iii) We have a responsibility to acquire some experience before making confident pronouncements, to earn some authority for our value judgments. And we must accord others some authority, too. Imagine Vizzini will not listen to others' claims about the movie, or to their reasons in support of their claims, because he considers their judgments irrelevant. If he is not open to correction from others, treating them as having some authority, too, then we might charge him with slipping back into thinking that the way he feels about something settles whether the movie is fantastic.

We need to discipline our claims about value in all these ways, to keep up a healthy practice of sharing value judgments. Let's call the various dispositions to discipline one's claims in all these important ways, *the dispositions to signal cooperatively.* A disposition is an inclination, or a tendency to act a certain way. If you are a reasonable person, you will have the dispositions we've just talked about: You'll be inclined to discipline your claims about value; you'll acknowledge the possibility of error on your own part, accept responsibility for what you have said or judged, estimate your reliability before issuing judgments, and accord others some authority in judging what is of value.

Why will you be inclined in all these ways? Because you're concerned to get it right about value. You know that other people might help you learn what is of value, if you listen. You also want others to get it right about value, so you are careful not to mislead. Their tracking value is a good thing. Your reliability as a judge of value is important to others as well as yourself. These concerns lead to dispositions to signal cooperatively about value.

These same dispositions also help us to learn about value—and not just about aesthetic value. Take a value such as *being credible.* If a claim is *credible* then there is evidence or reasons for it. Credibility is an epistemic value—a credible claim has positive worth, when it comes to gaining knowledge. Some claims are credible, and some are not. We are not born knowing the difference. Learning to distinguish the credible from the non-credible, or the downright incredible, takes concerted effort. Here is an example: Imagine Inez feels comfortable with the idea that humans are importantly different from other animals because they have souls, while other animals do not. Suppose this idea appeals to her because it has nice practical effects for her; it seems to Inez to explain why eating meat is morally permissible. Her felt comfort with the idea bears no relation to its *credibility*; put another way, felt comfort with an idea doesn't do anything to prove that the idea is true. To be a good epistemic agent (a good believer), Inez must learn to separate the *credibility* of her ideas from the comfort they produce.

Now suppose Inez is reasonable. She is inclined to signal cooperatively. These dispositions will help her to learn about *credibility.* Suppose Inez says, "It's credible that humans are importantly different from other animals because they have souls while other animals don't." Inez will listen to others, accord them some authority, and accept correction from them when they say things like "It's only credible if something speaks in favor of its truth—what reasons do you have for thinking your claim is true?" If others explain the difference between comfort and credibility, and their explanations are good, Inez will ultimately learn to track the features that make a claim credible.

Learning about value is not a solo venture. The development of Inez's ability to judge the presence of *credibility* comes not just through paying attention to her own history of classifying things, but also through paying attention to others' judgments, holding herself responsible to their criticisms, and accepting positive and negative feedback. The dispositions of a reasonable person don't just help us share value judgments; they help us learn about value. Not just epistemic value, but aesthetic value, moral value, and so on.[6]

What we've been talking about is how humans manage to be reasonable and map value together. We've been investigating the specific psychological traits, tendencies, or dispositions that make shared value-mapping possible. You don't have to miraculously step outside your point of view to share judgments of value. You do have to possess specific social dispositions to interact with others and specific inclinations to improve the reliability of your value judgments given what others think.

Let's apply our account of reasonableness to a real-life disagreement.

New York City scheduled its mayoral election for December 2001. As the September 11 attack on the World Trade Center threw the city into chaos, then-mayor Rudolph W. Giuliani expressed his desire to extend his term. Up against legal term limits, he summoned the mayoral candidates to his command center and told them he wanted a three-month extension, and if they did not agree, he might test the city's laws and run again despite the law forbidding his serving again. "I'm being reasonable," he said. "My supporters want me to run again" (Steinhauer 2001).

Others thought differently about the reasonableness of Giuliani's idea. Then-governor George E. Pataki later recounted that as he listened to Giuliani's plea for him to wield executive powers to extend his term, "my mind raced." Pataki thought to himself, "Are you really, right now, after a terror attack on our state, our city, asking me to just cancel the entire election? I am a conservative. We respect the law. For God's sake, you're a prosecutor! You know the law" (Golding 2020).

Giuliani and Pataki disagreed about what was reasonable, and they disagreed about who was being reasonable. Giuliani defended *efficiency* in a time of crisis as the most important value. Pataki defended the *rule of law* as the most important value. Which of them was right? What was the reasonable thing to do in this situation—delay the election or run it as scheduled? Who was being reasonable—Giuliani or Pataki, or both, or neither?

I won't try to answer these substantive questions about who is reasonable. That depends on further information that I do not have. What I will do instead is use the case to examine how to answer such questions. What sort of further information do we need?

As we have seen, a reasonable person is concerned to get it right about value. They're consequently critically minded and open-minded about value judgments, and they want good reasons for their beliefs about value. Further, they tend to talk to each other about value and disvalue in a cooperative way; they take responsibility for their value judgments, holding themselves to a standard beyond their personal preferences or impressions, and they accord others some authority about what is of value. They try to improve the reliability of their value judgments over time.

Whether Giuliani was being reasonable in his bid to delay the election depends on whether his judgment was a product of these qualities. Did his bid spring from a concern to get it right about value? In making his plea to stay in office was he manifesting dispositions to cooperatively track value? If we are interested in who is being reasonable, our task becomes that of answering these further questions. We have ways of discerning whether someone is concerned to get it right about what matters, ways of testing for the presence of the relevant dispositions.

For instance, Pataki thought it obvious that the rule of law is a greater value than governmental efficiency in a time of crisis. He would acknowledge governmental efficiency in a time of crisis is a good thing, but he judged the value of the rule of law obviously greater than that of efficiency, and he believed that Giuliani should have had no trouble making the same comparative judgment. Anyone with a law degree, Pataki believed, would see the overriding importance of the rule of law. Now, Hume notes if the relative importance of competing values is obvious, "no one pays attention" to an incorrect value judgment. It is like someone pronouncing "a mole-hill to be as high as Teneriffe or a pond as extensive as the ocean." Hume is right that we dismiss crazy value judgments; but he's wrong to say we pay no attention to them. We do pay attention to "absurd and ridiculous" value judgments. Some of our disagreements about value are such that obviously correct judgments become tests for the competence and sincerity of a person's judgment.

In cases where a value judgment is obvious, even in the absence of information about a person's dispositions, we can only assume that if they deny the obvious, they are biased, or moved by self-interest, or the like. If we have good reason to believe the person is a competent judge, then if we find their judgment absurd and ridiculous, we rule out mistake and look for motives. Pataki, following this line of reasoning, might naturally think Giuliani could not really believe that efficiency is of greater importance than the rule of law (for heaven's sake!), so something else lies behind his desire to delay the election. Consequently, he might see in Giuliani's claim about governmental efficiency a ploy to stay in power.

Pataki might check this judgment further. Giuliani appears to believe he is being reasonable. Now, we've already seen that this belief isn't enough to make him reasonable. He should care to have good reasons for his belief in the greater importance of efficiency in a time of crisis. Here, what he actually said in defense of the reasonableness of his position leaves something to be desired: "My supporters want me to run again" does not speak to the question of the relative importance of government efficiency as compared to the rule of law. And that is what he should be seeking to justify, if he is reasonable. The claim that his supporters wanted him to run is neither here nor there. If Giuliani was sincere in his belief that efficiency mattered more than the rule of law, his failure to take even the first steps to competently defend this claim leaves Pataki's hypothesis about Giuliani's motives in place. The most generous among us could say only "He was *trying* to be reasonable."

It is worth noting that when anyone says "I'm being reasonable," this is itself a value judgment. Being *reasonable* is a valuable thing. Giuliani should only make this claim if he disciplines his use of "reasonable" so that it does not merely mean in his mouth something like "I approve of how I'm thinking about things." He should be ready to accord others some authority over whether he applies the term "reasonable" correctly. His feeble attempt to defend the reasonableness of his bid ("my supporters want me to run again") suggests he may also have a weak grasp on what it means to be reasonable.

Giuliani eventually dropped his bid to postpone the election. Was he brought around by Pataki's reasons, freshly reminded of the importance of the rule of law and respecting regular elections? Was he brought up short when Pataki called him unreasonable, reminding him that there is substantive content to the word "reasonable"? Or did he see the writing on the wall—that is, did he see that his bid was not getting traction, and that it would be politically expedient to drop the idea? (Were that the case, he did the reasonable thing, but he was not reasonable in doing it.)

It can be hard to answer such questions. But it is not impossible. We can gather evidence about whether two people are having a reasonable disagreement. A reasonable disagreement is a disagreement between reasonable people who make different, though justified, value judgments. We identify unreasonable disagreement by finding deficient reasoning, bias, or the absence of dispositions to discipline one's value judgments (to signal cooperatively about value). Imagine that Giuliani is ready to defend his belief that his term as Mayor should be extended. He cites good reasons (maybe former cases where a new administration struggled to come up to speed while dealing with an unprecedented crisis, and consequently people's health and safety suffered); and suppose he defends his comparative evaluative judgment, saying, "The rule of law is of course important, but never more important than even a single human life." Imagine that Pataki is similarly ready to defend his beliefs with good reasons and engage in cooperative discussion of the comparative value of the rule of law as against the efficiency of government ("even if some individuals are made to suffer, the rule of law guarantees more people safety"). If they both have some significant justification for their value judgments and are willing to talk cooperatively about their competing evaluations, acknowledging the possibility of error on their own part, accepting responsibility for what they say ("I'm being reasonable—here's why"), and according others some authority in judging what is of value, then we might reasonably hold that their disagreement is reasonable.

Being reasonable, you know that reasonable disagreements about value can happen. (People have what Hume calls "opposite sentiments.") And you know we can also disagree about whether a disagreement is reasonable or not. If you are reasonable, you will be concerned to spot the difference. The difference depends on two main things: the presence of dispositions to discipline one's value judgments and the presence of justification—reasons and evidence—in support of one's value judgments. How do we tell if a person has the relevant dispositions? Being ready to talk about value cooperatively is some evidence. How readily does the person accept responsibility for their claims, and how seriously do they take the questions asking them to explain why they think what they do? Does the person have good reasons for their judgments and are they concerned to communicate them clearly? These are all things we can make reasoned judgments about. So we can make reasoned judgments about whether a disagreement is reasonable or not.

Our vigorous disagreements about value do not threaten the very possibility of sharing a map of the value landscape. Trying for a shared map makes a lot of sense. It is important to get it right about value, and sometimes it is tricky to get it right about value, so sharing our impressions is vital. Where we cannot get agreement, if we can at least agree that our disagreement is reasonable, then we can at least mark our shared map with a notation about the lack of agreement: “Here there be monsters.”

We often share and contest our value judgments. We share and contest because we are social, and we share all kinds of beliefs and information. We want others to find what’s good, worthy, and valuable while avoiding the harmful, nasty stuff. But it is not just that we are inveterate sharers of information. There is a deeper fact: We want to get it right about important things, and doing so is often a joint endeavor. As Hume notes, we arrive at the very terms we use to express value judgments through interaction and conversation with others—reasonable others, that is, people who are responsive to others’ perspectives. We also learn about and refine our grasp on value through interaction with others. Mapping the value landscape is a social endeavor, calling for social qualities that are fundamental to being reasonable. The reasonable person is not a lone cartographer.

6

Reasonable Emotion

Why is it hard to be reasonable? Emotions can make it difficult. Raw feelings can overwhelm you and make you lose track of what matters. But your emotions can also be a way for you to learn about your environment. They can tell you what to seek—the helpful, beneficial, and advantageous things—and what to avoid—the repugnant, disgusting, and harmful things. Say you are visiting an unfamiliar city, finding your way to your hotel, and suddenly you feel uneasy about the street ahead. Time to turn around, you think. Why? You might not find it easy to say—you might just have an anxious feeling. Or say you meet someone and feel instantly comfortable with them. What a great person, you think. Maybe it's not easy to say what exactly it is about them—you just have a good feeling. Emotions can encode lots of information about value. Your anger informs you of insults and other rips in the social fabric; fear informs you of potential harm, social and physical; joy informs you of singular, special goods. Emotions are important tools for discovering value in our environment.

The problem is that emotions can also mislead you. Walking in a strange city, you see and hear unfamiliar sights and sounds that do not correlate with danger at all. Entering a new relationship, the rush of delight may blot out other emotions and cloud one's thinking. Some emotions are indiscriminate—they fire away, often mistakenly. Fear and anger notoriously seem to be hardwired this way.[1] We might explain indiscriminate emotions, saying their job is to save you from danger; if fear alerts you to trouble when trouble is present, it has done its job. This explanation does not diminish the point that indiscriminate emotions can be highly misleading. And emotions can mislead in other ways, beyond being indiscriminate. They can capture and hold your attention to the exclusion of other important things, making you hyperfocused; they can be influenced by your mood, your background beliefs, and your physical state. If you are hungry, you may anger more easily than if you're full, if you are drunk you may find things funny that aren't. Emotions may also spur you to rationalize in self-deceptive ways—for example, if your anger causes you to search for reasons to be angry, and finding none, you invent some.

All this is fodder for loads of psychological research. Social psychologists study how emotions mislead us about the world, neuroscientists study how the presence (and absence) of emotion can make us worse reasoners, and behavioral psychologists study how we can modify our emotions with the practical aim of living happier lives.

How can we learn about value and disvalue from our emotions? Given the many powerful ways emotions can mislead us, this is a pressing question. I suggest we can learn from our emotions if they are reasonable. A reasonable person is concerned to get it right about value. So, a reasonable person regulates their emotions in several ways to fight the influence of misleading factors.

The idea that we might regulate our emotional responses has a long history. The Stoic philosopher Seneca (4 BCE–65 CE) laments unregulated emotions and encourages us to strive to replace our emotions with calmer responses.[2] Why feel anger over your house being burgled? asks Seneca—you cannot control being burgled, even with a fancy security system. Better to have a dispassionate response to the burglary, say, by forming an intention to pursue justice against the thief. I will suggest a similar point: We should strive to have reasonable emotions, not just to lead a calmer life, but to be better at discovering what matters.

We know that some of our emotions are reasonable. If a thief steals your stuff, it is reasonable to be angry. If a politician lies, it is reasonable to be disgusted. If your child succeeds after a long struggle, it is reasonable to feel enormously happy. Not feeling happy might signal you have a problem.[3] It's common sense that our emotions can be reasonable. But emotions mislead, too. Seneca identifies typical causes of misleading emotions, taking the example of anger. What causes many cases of anger? Seneca answers: "Money . . . the greatest hullabaloo is about money." He lists a few other causes, too:

> Let us enumerate the other causes of anger: they are food, drink, and the showy apparatus connected with them, words, insults, disrespectful movements of the body, suspicions, obstinate cattle, lazy slaves, and spiteful construction put upon other men's words, so that even the gift of language to mankind becomes reckoned among the wrongs of nature. Believe me, the things which cause us such great heat are trifles, the sort of things that children fight and squabble over: there is nothing serious, nothing important in all that we do with such gloomy faces. It is, I repeat, the setting a great value on trifles that is the cause of your anger and madness. (Seneca 1900)

On Seneca's view, anger ultimately owes to "setting a great value on trifles." On his view, only virtue matters—everything else is a trifle. So, feeling angry about anything other than failures of virtue is a mistake. On my view, many things matter—not just virtue. So, feeling angry about many things can be reasonable. On my view, anger does not always or only arise from "setting great value on trifles": sometimes it involves setting exactly the right amount of value on things that matter. And sometimes anger is reasonable. The same is true for other emotions.

Let's take an example. Chris Sale, starting pitcher for the Boston Red Sox, pitched a minor-league rehab game against the Scranton RailRiders, and it did not go well. He allowed a bases-loaded walk (a disaster for a pitcher), and the manager pulled him early from the game. Sale, who was fighting his way back from injury, was monumentally frustrated. News footage of him destroying the locker room circulated widely after the game. He tore a television from the wall and kicked it across the room. Commentators clucked about his behavior. Chaim Bloom, chief baseball officer for the team, defended Sale: "Look, I'm not going to sit here and condone property damage, but he is a competitor. That's who he is. So, it's never something that we condone, but there's a lot of passion in this game, and when you have someone who holds himself to as high a standard as Chris does and who cares as much as he does, sometimes that passion is going to express itself in different ways" (Chiari, "Red Sox's Chris Sale Damages Locker Room").

Like most emotions, frustration is a complex thing. Contemporary emotion researchers, including psychologists, neuroscientists, and philosophers, are moving to a consensus about the broad features of emotions: Each type of emotion has a distinctive profile of typical physiological (activation/deactivation), experiential (pleasure/displeasure), and behavioral elements.[4] If you're angry, typically your heart rate goes up, you feel agitated and displeased, and you tend to act with aggression. If you're sad, typically you feel less energetic, displeased, and tend to withdraw from contact with others. Second, emotions represent the world around us. If someone slights us, we react to the slight with anger. The anger represents the slight—it carries the information *that was a slight!* Third, emotions often depend on our beliefs. Chris Sale only got frustrated because he believed that he was pitching poorly. If he hadn't thought this, he would not have been frustrated. Finally, emotions do not just represent the world: they also involve an evaluation of it. You are joyful at your friend's winning the lottery—your joy evaluates their win as a wonderful thing. You are also envious—your envy evaluates their win as something desirable that you lack.

Let's use this consensus account to dive into what it takes for an emotion to be reasonable. Imagine coming home and seeing the broken doorframe of your house, and as you enter, you also notice your wallet and keys are missing. Fear wells up in you. But imagine the case filled in this way: Your house hasn't been robbed; your teenage son forgot his keys, and so he pried the lock. He proceeded to borrow both your money and the car. In this case, even if your fear is mistaken (there is no danger), we still want to say your fear is reasonable. It is based on justified beliefs, and it fits the situation you justifiably believe yourself to be in. If instead the case is one where you routinely fear break-ins, and the mere sense that your porch looks different than it did when you left in the morning triggers a fear that you have been burgled, then your fear might fit the situation you believe yourself to be in, but your fear fails to be reasonable: The belief it is based on is unjustified—there is plenty of evidence that no break-in has occurred. In such a case, we might hunt for a cause (maybe past trauma) and describe your fear as understandable, or forgivable, but not reasonable.

Emotions are evaluations of your situation. To be reasonable, your emotion needs to be well grounded—that is, based on justified beliefs—fitting for the situation you justifiably believe yourself to be in, and appropriate in scale. A reasonable person is concerned to get it right about value; and emotions that are well grounded, fitting, and appropriately scaled tend to be correct evaluations of their circumstances.

Let's return to Chris Sale's frustration. Many fans were ready to judge Sale as unreasonable. (After the incident, the Red Sox Reddit filled with complaints: he was "a baby" who threw "a tantrum.") Let's think about how Sale's frustration could have been reasonable. Note that we are not talking about whether his *actions* were reasonable: Everyone might agree that it was not reasonable for Sale to trash the locker room. Reasonable emotions can cause unreasonable actions. The law recognizes this distinction: The act of killing someone is not reasonable, but the fear that drove you to kill might be reasonable. We are just focusing on whether Sale's frustration was reasonable. Frustration points to an obstacle on the way to a goal. Sale's frustration was based on a justified belief: he had good grounds for believing his bad pitching would block his goal of returning to the Major League. This was not his first loss in his rehabilitation, and this loss made his return to the roster look especially doubtful. His frustration was fitting—his goal of returning to the Majors was blocked by his bad performance on the mound. Was his affect appropriately scaled to what he believed about the disvalue in his situation? His frustration was monumental. Was this level of affect appropriate considering what he justifiably believed about his situation? Arguably yes: His goal of returning to the Majors mattered a lot—it meant continuing a storied career, living up to the expectations of millions of devoted fans, and holding up his side of a multimillion-dollar contract. His failure in the rehab game was evidence of the permanent loss of an extraordinary athletic gift. With all that at stake, a high level of frustration was appropriate. Had he been mildly annoyed, that would have been inappropriate. Given his situation, Sale's frustration seems reasonable.

But wait, someone might say, wouldn't it be better for Sale to remain calm? It might be better for him to follow Seneca's advice and recognize what matters in his situation (that his pitching needs improvement) without feeling so very much. His relations with his teammates and fans might improve, and his blood pressure might be healthier, too. Seneca's advice has appeal: In many cases, not feeling so much might be good for us. However, there are empirical questions here about human emotion that must be answered before one can say that Seneca's advice is good. Can we reliably achieve freedom from powerful emotion while we recognize the full import of what matters in our situation? Some emotions involve strong motivations to act. Could a perfectly calm Sale be motivated to the degree necessary to put in the long hours and hard work to improve his pitching? If not, then his best course might be to work on being reasonable, which will keep his frustration justified, fitting, and appropriate in scale.

How can we ensure our emotions are reasonable? Several dispositions or inclinations help us put a check on the factors that produce misleading emotions. We have already seen one such disposition—namely, the disposition to accord others authority about value and to take correction from others about what's valuable—the disposition to signal cooperatively.

Here is a case to illustrate. Imagine a Sunday softball league player feels monumentally frustrated by a loss—as frustrated as Sale—and he destroys a locker room. Imagine he says in his defense, "Look, I'm a competitor, that's who I am. There's a lot of passion in this game, and sometimes my passion just expresses itself this way." We need to know more about his situation to determine whether his frustration is reasonable. Before passing judgment, we want to know how and why the game matters to him, and what he believes about his situation. Has he bet his house on how well he pitches in this game? (An unreasonable action, perhaps, but given this action, his emotion might be reasonable.) Is he vying for a spot on a World Softball Championship team, and a scout is in the stands? Let's fill in the case this way: It is an ordinary Sunday league game, with nothing riding on the outcome; because there are so few players in the league who can pitch at all, his position as pitcher is secure, no matter how badly he plays; his playing well in a Sunday game has the importance that any skillful activity pursued for fun might have. In this case, he is taking things too hard, and he shouldn't be so very frustrated. His emotion misrepresents things—it is either not well-grounded or out of scale, or both.

Now imagine the Sunday player is fundamentally reasonable, and he tends to accord others authority about value and to take correction from them about what is valuable. His frustration incorporates a value judgement, and since he is reasonable, he does not suppose that this judgment answers only to his preferences or his own point of view. Defending his monumental frustration, he might say "It mattered a lot to me!" but he will also accept responsibility to state reasons for thinking that the loss mattered a lot. He understands he ought to have some reasons for this value judgment ("It mattered a lot because . . ."). He accords others authority about what matters and why. If his teammates challenge him, "what is so important about this game?" he will be disposed to try to answer them, and if he cannot answer, he will tend to correct his evaluation. Since he does not take himself to be the only judge of whether the reasons he comes up with are good ones, he won't merely rationalize his frustration, coming up with just any reason. This is how a reasonable person tempers their frustration.

The Sunday player might have come by his unreasonable frustration in several ways. He might have grown up in a home where athletic failure was disgraceful, so he reacts this way to losing a game, or he might believe that his self-worth requires excellence in everything he does. There are many social, cultural, and psychological factors that shape our emotions. Some of these factors make our emotions unreasonable—unjustified or out of proportion. If one is reasonable, one's disposition to cooperate about value judgments helps put a check on the effects of such factors and so tamps down unreasonable emotions.

Let's look at other dispositions that help us put a check on unreasonable emotions.

The philosopher Michael Brady (2014) notes that emotions capture and consume our attention. Attention capture can be good, Brady argues, because keeping your attention on the object of your emotion can give you time to inquire into why you feel as you do. But Brady also warns that emotions can capture attention in ways that harm us. First, emotion can lead to attention that persists, long after it should dissipate, and persisting attention can lead to excessive reflection. For example, his bad pitches capture the Sunday player's attention; he keeps replaying them in his mind. Second, persisting attention can in turn lead to a search for reasons that confirm one's initial emotional response. The Sunday player might come to think this game must matter more than any other, simply because he keeps thinking about it. Third, negative emotions can also narrow one's attention on the emotional object to the exclusion of other important things in one's environment. The Sunday player's frustration consumes all his attention, so he does not notice the way he persevered, or the way his teammates appreciated his endurance.

How can one fight these misallocations of attention? Imagine that the Sunday player is reasonable. His concern is to have an accurate and sharable map of the value landscape. This concern generates dispositions or inclinations—including the disposition to allocate attention, so as not to get stuck on one thing, but to spread his attention to be alive to the whole of his situation. If the Sunday player is inclined to spread his attention, he won't excessively return in his mind to his bad pitching. Consequently, excessive reflection won't cause him to think his pitching must matter a lot, because he won't in fact attend to it excessively. Moreover, if he tends to spread his attention, he will not narrow his focus to his negative performance—the number of bad pitches—but he will instead register other kinds of value in his situation, such as camaraderie, sportsmanship, and the joy of physical play. Excessive attention and reflection would inhibit his progress in mapping the value landscape as a whole, and so he's disposed not to hyperfocus. The disposition to spread his attention makes the Sunday player a better value-mapper—not only a more accurate value-mapper, but a more cooperative one, too. Spreading one's attention to map the whole value landscape in one's situation means one's judgments will be of use to others. The Sunday player's teammates need him to notice other important values in his situation.

Being reasonable means being concerned about the accuracy and shareability of one's value judgments. This concern gives rise to specific dispositions: to avoid biased beliefs, to accord others authority about value and to take correction from them about what is valuable, to not allow one's attention to persist in unhelpful ways—to not become hyperfocused, but to spread one's attention and remain alive to the whole of one's situation. These dispositions serve to make one's emotions reasonable: They help one to be sensitive to good grounds for one's emotions, and to keep one's emotions fitting and proportionate to one's circumstances.

We have been looking into the mind of a reasonable person, into the dispositions that help reasonable people reliably track value together. Before moving on, I want to make one more point about the psychology of a reasonable person. It's often noted that it is hard to change one's emotions by reasoning. Imagine you find yourself frozen with fear at the Grand Canyon Skywalk, unable to step out onto the glass floor with its view of the canyon bottom thousands of feet below. You might find yourself unable to calm your fears no matter how emphatically you affirm to yourself the facts about its safety. Where conscious reasoning fails to help correct emotion, emotion can step in to help correct emotion (Goldie 2008). Reasonableness itself involves emotion—it involves being concerned or caring that one's appraisals of value are accurate and sharable with others. Being concerned for something means being emotionally engaged by it (Chapter 4). If you are concerned for your safety, you have relevant emotions about your safety. If you are concerned to form accurate beliefs about value, then you are emotionally engaged by a goal—the goal of getting it right about value. So, being reasonable involves an epistemic emotion. It involves caring to accurately track value, in all its many forms. The emotional side of being reasonable can help fight misleading emotions. I'm not saying reasonableness is an easy fix for our recalcitrant emotions. In the tug-of-war among our emotions, all sorts of further psychological factors will influence which emotion wins out. I am saying that a concern to get it right about value involves an emotion, one that can help prevent your attention from hyperfocusing on the view of the canyon below, and help you switch your attention to the beauty of the view.

Some emotions that might have troubled Seneca are, on my view, reasonable: Chris Sale's frustration, your disgust at the lying politician, your elation at your kid's overcoming a hurdle. And on my view, some emotions are never reasonable. Schadenfreude, for instance. You are not tracking value accurately and cooperatively if you take joy in another's sorrow. What about envy? Is it ever reasonable to be envious? The answer depends on how we characterize envy. Earlier, I suggested that envy might be a reasonable reaction to your friend's winning the lottery. I took it that envy informs you of something desirable that you lack. Call this the innocent view of envy. The philosopher Aaron Ben-Ze'ev (1990, 491) suggests a less innocent view, writing, "The focus of concern in envy is the subject's inferiority in relation to another agent." Suppose Zadie envies Arlo for his new sports car. It's fast and powerful. She wants to have what he has, maybe not *his* car, but a car as nice as his. By itself, such a desire seems innocent enough. Envy, though, is more than this desire, says Ben-Ze'ev. Envy is also about the social comparison that the car induces. Paul Bloom, psychologist, concurs with Ben-Ze'ev (Bloom, "Envy"):

> The envious feeling when a friend wins a great prize isn't just
>
> > *that bastard I hate him so much he gets everything and I get nothing*
>
> it's also
>
> > *everyone thinks I'm a loser*

Social comparison is the heart of envy, according to Bloom and Ben-Ze'ev. Zadie feels the sting of a social comparison that reflects poorly on her: why hasn't she managed to get such a car?

If this is all that envy whispers in our ear, then its reasonableness depends on whether the stinging social comparison is well grounded. The belief that someone else's accomplishment reflects poorly on oneself might have some justification. One can sensibly ask oneself, "why have I, with all the same resources, not pulled off the success this other person has managed?" But we can also find in Ze'ev's characterization an added twist. Envy, he seems to suggest, is not just about social comparison but also about its unfairness, and a desire that the unfairness be righted. If that were the case, then what lies at the heart of Zadie's envy is her belief that she is in a socially inferior position to Arlo—the sports car shows her up—and the belief that her inferior position is unfair or undeserved, and the desire that this wrong be righted. Arlo doesn't deserve a sports car—not more than she does, anyway, and this unfairness should be redressed. If this view of envy is correct, envy is, like schadenfreude, not reasonable. "If you would just not succeed, I would not suffer the unflattering comparison to you" can be a true thought, but it is inadequate justification for desiring another person's loss of something good. This desire is only justified in special conditions. One might desire that a person be stripped of some good because, say, their goals or their means of attaining it were immoral. In the absence of such special conditions, a person's possessing a good brings something of value into the world, and a reasonable person sees this as a good thing.

It is interesting that we do not find "reasonable envy" an excuse in the law. The law does, however, posit reasonable fear as an excuse that helps mitigate a wrongful act. But not just any emotion can serve as an excuse. Imagine Zadie steals Arlo's car. "I was envious—reasonably enough," she says in her defense. No judge will take her envy as a mitigating factor in assessing her crime. Envy of the strong kind, that wants the balance evened, is never reasonable.

A final topic—one of our themes—is the possibility of disagreement among reasonable people. There are limits on reasonable divergence in our emotions, set by the nature of reasonable emotion itself. For instance, cruelty is bad, and no one can reasonably be happy about cruel acts; so there can be no reasonable disagreement where one person is happy about an instance of cruelty while another person abhors it. But there are plenty of instances of reasonable divergence in our emotions. In the simplest instance, we differ in our emotions because we have limited emotional resources. If you're excited about our vacation and I am just too tired to muster enthusiasm, the divergence in our emotions is reasonable and explicable; it does not owe to a failure on anyone's part to get it right about value. Like you, I can think the vacation is a great idea. Our difference in our emotional reaction owes merely to our differing levels of psychic energy.

Things get more interesting when we diverge in our emotions because our evaluations conflict. The value landscape is open to competing depictions, and our individual maps of value can fail to align. So, our emotions can reasonably differ. But as reasonable people, we sometimes feel pressure toward coherence among our emotions. A reasonable emotion in one person can place demands on the emotions of other reasonable people.

To see how this works, let's start by considering this case from the philosopher Agnes Callard:

> Suppose that you are angry on Tuesday because I stole from you on Monday. Suppose that on Wednesday I return what I stole; I compensate you for any disadvantage occasioned by your not having had it for two days; I offer additional gifts to show my good will; I apologize for my theft as a moment of weakness; and, finally, I promise never to do it again. Suppose, in addition, that you believe my apology is sincere and that I will keep my promise.[5]

The question Callard puts to us is whether it could be reasonable for you to be as angry on Thursday as you were on Tuesday. To flesh out the case, suppose your anger at Agnes on Tuesday is reasonable. Suppose Agnes steals a sweater from you on Monday, and she does so because she simply wants your sweater—there are no mitigating circumstances; she has no need for the sweater, and no second thoughts about what she is doing, or how it will affect you.

Callard acknowledges that we typically think bearing a grudge after apologies, compensation of your loss, and additional gifts, is unreasonable. But, she insists:

> There are reasons to remain angry. And the reasons are not hard to find: they are the same reasons as the reasons to get angry in the first place. Apologies, restitution, and all the rest do nothing to cancel or alter the fact that I stole, nor the fact that I ought not to have stolen. Those facts were your reasons to be angry. Since they are not changed by my forms of redress—apology, compensation, what have you—then you still have, after the deployment of these amends, the very same reasons to be angry.

Anger, according to Callard, is an emotion that registers a harmful event, an event that is just as fixed in space-time as the extinction of the dinosaurs: "What I did will always diverge from what I ought to have done," she says, "no matter what I do *next*." If the reason for your anger remains, Callard argues, so should your anger continue, settling into a grudge: "Once you have a reason to be angry, you have a reason to be angry forever."

Callard's position goes against common sense. On Thursday your anger is not reasonable. We can say more about why: The reasonableness of an emotion has to do with how well it tracks value and disvalue in one's situation; your anger now, after Agnes has done so much to make amends, fails to track important value and disvalue.

Her making amends and seeking to restore goodwill on Wednesday is valuable. If you are a reasonable person, you will respond to these facts and at least soften your anger.

So, Callard's case does not support her claim that grudges are reasonable. We can find a more interesting moral in the case, though. The case demonstrates the way a reasonable emotion in one person can place demands on the emotions of other reasonable people. To see how, let's think more about anger.

In a famous article, the philosopher Peter Strawson (1962) identifies an important class of emotions—anger, resentment, gratitude, compunction, remorse, and respect—that he calls the "reactive attitudes." What makes these attitudes special is that they involve *a reaction to other people's attitudes.* "Reactive attitudes are essentially natural human reactions to the good or ill will or indifference of others toward us, as displayed in their attitudes and actions," Strawson writes. He adds that we generally expect "a reasonable degree of goodwill or regard, on the part of others" and, importantly, not simply toward ourselves, "but towards all those on whose behalf moral indignation may be felt" (1962, 200). Say Agnes steals a sweater from you on Monday, and—fleshing out the case—she does so without any mitigating thoughts such as "I wish I didn't have to do this"; she simply wants your sweater. She thereby makes clear her lack of goodwill toward you. Your anger is not just over your loss; it is over her attitude of indifference to you. A bystander witnessing all this also feels something on your behalf—indignation, disappointment—because the bystander, too, expects a reasonable degree of goodwill from Agnes toward you.

The philosopher Bennett Helm adds to Strawson's story about reactive attitudes a further claim: Our reactive attitudes are "rationally related" to each other. Within a single person, it only makes sense to feel *relieved* if what one *feared* doesn't transpire, or to feel *happy* when something one *cares* about is promoted in some way. Helm claims one individual's emotions are similarly connected to other people's emotions: "What reactive emotions it is rational for me to feel are tied to those it is rational for others to feel" (Helm 2014, 48). For example, your anger at Agnes on Tuesday is "rationally connected" to the bystander's indignation, which is in turn rationally connected to Agnes's guilt.

Helm is onto something important here about the way our emotions relate to each other, but it is not clear what exactly he means by "rational," so it is not clear how rationality forges ties among our emotions. We also need to be careful about the strength of the interpersonal ties among our emotions. We can reasonably differ in our emotions. So, it is not right to say that there is one and only one thing for me to feel and that it is causally or rationally determined by your feelings. That would be too strong a tie.

We can say reasonableness forges ties among our emotions, in the following sense: one person's reasonable reactive emotions can place a defeasible normative pressure on the reactive emotions of others. Start with the interpersonal case. If you are reasonable—an adept value-mapper—your emotions register value and disvalue around you. Your emotions will consequently evolve coherently as circumstances change. You care about your friend's well-being, so if you find out she is in peril you will be anxious; if you find out she's safe, your anxiety will give way to relief. It only makes sense that your anxiety gives way to relief. If you are reasonable, your emotions track the prospects of the things you value through changing circumstances, and so your emotions tend to relate to each other in a sensible, coherent fashion.

If you are reasonable, your reactive emotions will also tend to relate coherently to the emotions of other reasonable people. For example, I take a second cup of coffee, draining the pot, even though I know you have not yet had your morning cup. You are miffed. My action shows a lack of goodwill toward you—or at least a problematic indifference. Your mild anger is reasonable: It is well grounded (based on justified beliefs), fitting for the situation you justifiably believe yourself to be in, and appropriate in scale; it tracks something of disvalue, namely, my lack of concern for you. If the anger you feel is reasonable, then there is some pressure on me to feel guilt (embarrassment, compunction) and pressure on a witness to my act to feel indignation (disappointment, disapproval) on your behalf. We are responding to the same event—my taking the last cup—and the value and disvalue it brings into the world. If you reasonably feel a reactive emotion (anger), then other things being equal, it will be reasonable for others to feel corresponding emotions (guilt, indignation).

The pressure to feel corresponding emotions is defeasible—further facts about our circumstances may mean we reasonably differ in our reactions. Suppose I do not feel guilty about taking the last cup. Guilt would be reasonable, given the reasonable anger you feel. But it is not required that I feel guilt, given the possibility of reasonable disagreement in our evaluative beliefs. Maybe we disagree at a fundamental level about the distribution of inessential goods such as coffee, or about the proper interpretation of actions and when exactly they reveal a lack of concern. Given that there can be reasonable disagreement about value and about the interpretation of our actions, we cannot say that I must feel guilt or compunction for doing what angers you. Your being miffed creates at most a defeasible normative pressure on me to respond with a corresponding reactive emotion. If I don't feel these things, some account of the discrepancy may be called for. (I might recognize you have good reason to be angry, but I'm emotionally overwhelmed by other, bigger issues in my life.)

People who try to track value together are disposed to accord each other authority about where value is to be found. So, a reasonable person is disposed to listen to the implicit claim made by someone else's anger (or to respond to the implicit approval in someone else's gratitude, and so forth). If you resent my taking the last cup of coffee, then if I am reasonable, I accept that your emotion may be an appropriate reaction to my act. This is why I am motivated to react in some way: either by feeling something (compunction) that coheres with your feeling (anger), or by explaining the discrepancy in our emotions.

Let's return to your holding a grudge against Agnes for her thievery. Recall that we've fleshed out the case a bit: Agnes stole your sweater, merely because she liked it, and without giving your needs or interests a second thought. While Agnes may regret what she did and continue to feel remorse ("what a stupid thing to do"), having reformed her ways and having acted to repair the damage, she can also feel good about herself. These feelings make feelings of unmitigated guilt on her part unreasonable. Similarly, a witness can move from feeling outright indignation at Agnes's thievery to feeling approval for her efforts to atone for her wrongdoing. These emotions are reasonable—they track the evolving landscape of value.

Agnes's pride at reforming herself and the witness's approval of her actions since Tuesday place defeasible demands on your emotions. If you accord others authority about value and are open to correction, you will reflect on your grudge. You might say to the witness, "Your approving attitude about Agnes is reasonable but so is my anger." As a reasonable person, you will then need to think more about what you are saying. Now you are talking about value, and the disposition to accord others authority about value and to take correction from others will have you searching for reasons and considering others' viewpoint on the action. If Agnes subsequently feels remorse, her emotion is also something you track, and if you're reasonable, you will see some value in her remorse—it is appropriate; it registers the wrong done to you, and it may cause better behavior in her next time. So, you will feel something about her remorse, too, a feeling of approval. Registering her efforts to make amends, somewhere along the line you may even forgive her.[6]

Reasonable emotions register value and disvalue in our lives. Unreasonable emotions mislead us. While conscious reasoning alone rarely has sufficient grip on us to combat powerful emotions, a concern to make accurate and shareable value judgments exerts a grip on us. This concern itself involves an emotion, specifically an epistemic emotion; and it generates various dispositions that make one's emotions more reasonable, more reliable guides to the value landscape. We know that people can reasonably diverge in their emotions. But some of our reasonable emotions make reasonable demands on others to respond with reasonable emotions of their own. Reasonable anger, for instance, exerts pressure on perpetrators to feel guilt, compunction, remorse and the like. We can resist such pressure because we can have reasonable disagreement in our evaluative judgments. Still, one needs to resist on good grounds—grounds that reasonable others can appreciate. The reasonableness of an emotion depends on how well it tracks value and disvalue cooperatively. In this way, reasonable emotions help us learn about value together.

7

Reasonable Belief

When Rodney Peairs shot and killed Yoshi Hattori, he believed that he had to use deadly force to save his own life. At his criminal trial, the sincerity of his belief was not in doubt. The question for the jury was whether his belief was reasonable. Judging his belief was reasonable, the criminal trial jury found Peairs not guilty.

What makes a belief reasonable? And what makes it possible to disagree about whether a belief is reasonable?

To start our inquiry, let's flip our question on its head: What can make a belief unreasonable? It turns out there are lots of things.

Lack of reasons or evidence can make one's belief unreasonable. (We can think of reasons as facts that make one's belief more likely to be true, and we can think of evidence as both physical objects such as a bloody glove, a knife—things one can place on the evidence table in a courtroom—and nonphysical things such as testimony.)[1] A simple example is wishful belief. Imagine a case: I have no reason to think I can get a big project finished by the deadline, but I believe I can, only because that happy thought reduces my anxiety. That a thought reduces my anxiety is not a reason to believe it is true. We can also imagine cases of biased belief: Imagine that Iago believes that Othello, a Moorish general of the Venetian army, is unfit for his position of authority and does not deserve the love of Desdemona; but Iago has a biased belief that is caused by his racism; it is not grounded in evidence of Othello's incompetence. We can call reasons or evidence the "grounds" of one's belief. Lack of grounds can make one's belief unreasonable.

Sometimes you have grounds, but they are not strong enough to support belief: For example, you have a scratchy throat—one symptom of Covid-19—but little exposure, and multiple tests are negative. You have some grounds for thinking you have Covid, but not enough to sustain a belief that you have Covid. (If your belief is out of proportion to your evidence, that is like being massively frustrated over failing to reach a goal that is insignificant.) In other cases, you have grounds that seem good, but further reflection reveals they are bad grounds: Say the roulette ball has landed on red the past twenty times, and you take that as reason to believe it will land on black this time (the gambler's fallacy). Readers can find compendia of such mistakes, where one suffers an illusion of good grounds.[2] Here is an interesting case of inadequate grounds that legal theorists discuss (Nesson 1979; Redmayne 2008):

> Prisoners in the Yard: 100 prisoners are out for their daily exercise in the prison yard. Suddenly, 99 of them execute a plan to attack the guards. One lone prisoner plays no role in the attack, knowing nothing about the plan. No cameras or eyewitnesses can help identify prisoners or the parts they played in the attack. Given the statistical evidence, it's 99% probable that prisoner Jones is guilty, so the warden picks Jones to punish.

The case is artificial—a pared-down thought experiment meant to focus our attention on the implications of forming our beliefs solely on the basis of statistical evidence. The warden's picking one person to punish raises moral issues of fairness, but legal theorists who use the case want to focus our attention on epistemic issues about the power of statistical evidence to support beliefs about individuals. If the warden is to believe that Jones is guilty, it must be on the basis of more individualized evidence, says Judith Jarvis Thomson. Writing about such cases, she remarks, "I strongly suspect that what people feel the lack of . . . is evidence which is in an appropriate way causally connected with the (putative) fact that the defendant caused the harm."[3] Although the probability that Jones took part in the attack is high, this statistical evidence lacks an important tie to Jones, a tie that would exist if, say, we were to see his face on closed-circuit television.

Another way your belief can turn unreasonable is your failing to use the good grounds you possess. Imagine Iago as described above, but this time he learns about Othello's exploits in battle and the success of the Venetian army under his command. Iago's informant is very credible, someone whom Iago is ready to believe about other matters. But Iago will not change his mind about Othello, still believing him unfit for his position of authority. Iago's belief is dogmatic—it does not change when he receives new evidence that he has good reason to accept. As credible new evidence comes in, a reasonable person changes their belief to accord with it.

You can also fail to acquire evidence that is there for the taking. If evidence is available, a reasonable person uses it.[4] Availability of evidence is an important feature in deciding whether a belief is reasonable.[5] Here is an example. It's morning and you head to the kitchen planning on making an omelet with cream cheese. You believe there is cream cheese in the fridge. You remember seeing the tub last night, and when you saw it, you formed your plan about breakfast. Your memory provides good grounds for your belief that there's cream cheese in the fridge. Now you enter the kitchen and stand in front of the refrigerator. Your roommate has left you a note, posted at eye level on the refrigerator door, and written in large red letters: *We Have No Cream Cheese—I used it all up!* You fail to see the note. You still believe there's cream cheese in the fridge, but you ought to know better. You should use all available evidence in forming your beliefs—no cherry-picking, and no missing what's obvious. One's belief is unreasonable if one fails to make use of all the available evidence.

When is evidence *available?* It comes very naturally to us to say "I should have known better," but when exactly is it right to say this? We might think the availability of evidence comes down to whether access to it is physically possible. But that won't do; it is physically possible for you to find out about the note on the fridge before you enter the kitchen (for example, it is physically possible to put a camera in the kitchen trained on the refrigerator, with a feed to your phone). This fact does not mean that you should have known better than to believe there was cream cheese in the fridge. Before you entered the kitchen, your belief was reasonable, even though it was physically possible to find out about the note. It was only after you stood in front of the fridge within inches of the highly salient note that your belief became unreasonable.

Another tempting idea is that the availability of evidence hinges upon what a person might discover through competently exercising typical human perceptual and cognitive powers. But this idea doesn't square with our judgments about reasonableness: Imagine a person whose perceptual disability means they don't see the note on the fridge. Will their belief that there is still cream cheese in the fridge count as *unreasonable?* That's not how we use the word "reasonable." Perhaps the best we can say is that evidence is available for a person when they are not lazy, careless, dogmatic, or inattentive, and are able to easily find it.[6] We allow some subject-relativity of what is available. This description of availability is rough, but it will serve our purposes.

Having a reasonable belief is a significant cognitive achievement. Reasonable belief is based on good reasons or evidence, only as firm as the evidence warrants, and free from bias, dogmatism, and carelessness. These are valuable qualities in a belief. They are varieties of *epistemic value*. The value of these qualities lies in two facts. First, beliefs that have these qualities are more likely to be true than beliefs that lack these qualities. Truth is something we want in a belief. You cannot get it right about value without getting it right about the facts—that is, without having true beliefs. Second, beliefs with these qualities are more likely to serve as the basis for cooperation with other reasonable people. A belief that is free of bias is more likely to be sharable with other reasonable people. We cannot get it right about value together without sharing some beliefs about the facts.

Let's return to Peairs's belief and consider the question of whether it was reasonable or not. First, a couple of clarifications: In this case, records show that both Peairs and an appeals court judge invoked *reasonable fear* and *reasonable belief* interchangeably. This makes sense. One's fear is only reasonable if one has *good grounds for believing* one is in danger. So, it is natural to move back and forth from talking about reasonable fear to claims about reasonable belief. Second, the law puts a specific belief under the microscope in cases of self-defense. The Louisiana law states: A *homicide is justifiable when committed in self-defense by one who reasonably believes that he is in imminent danger of losing his life or receiving great bodily harm and that the killing is necessary to save himself from that danger* (*Hattori v. Peairs* 1995). Peairs said in his defense that he believed that his life was in imminent danger and that killing was necessary to save himself. So, the question is whether this specific belief of his was reasonable. The belief has two components. We will look at each component separately and try to assess whether it is reasonable.

Let's start with Peairs's belief that he was in imminent danger. In a legal context, *imminent danger* means an immediate or present threat of death or grave physical harm. Was Peairs's belief about imminent danger reasonable? An obvious question is whether Hattori's race biased Peairs's belief. Cynthia Lee suggests that Hattori's race influenced the jury. There is evidence that Peairs and his wife Bonnie noted that Hattori looked different. The judge asked Bonnie to describe Hattori, and she said, "I guess he appeared oriental. He could have been Mexican or whatever" (Lee 2003, 169). Rodney Peairs said that he saw an oriental male, approximately five-foot seven, in the light of the carport. Lee writes:

> The fact that Hattori was a foreigner, a Japanese citizen and not an American, simply made it easier for the Baton Rouge jury to empathize with Peairs. They could picture themselves in Peairs's shoes. If an Asian teenager came onto their property and refused to freeze even with a gun pointed at his chest, that teenager was asking to be shot.

Lee adds that it is easy to imagine a jury judging a different case, where race was not a factor, very differently:

> Because of Hattori's nationality, the jurors couldn't see Hattori as one of their own sons. If Webb Haymaker, the boy from the neighborhood, had been the victim in this case, Peairs would have found it difficult to persuade the jury that he was terrified for his life and thought the boy looked like a crazy man. (Lee 2003, 169–170)

That the jury might have been biased doesn't speak directly to whether Peairs's belief about imminent danger was biased. And that is the question we're focusing on. Lee is suggesting that Peairs, just like his neighbors, found it easier to be terrified because Hattori was Asian. Courts have various means of trying to prevent biased beliefs from entering legal reasoning and judgments. Attorneys select juries from a pool, and they can challenge potential jurors for bias. Judges can instruct jurors, reminding them of the importance of not allowing personal bias to affect their reasoning. And attorneys can cross-examine defendants to try to uncover hidden biases in their thinking. (Juries can in some cases ask the defendant questions, too, though it depends on the jurisdiction.) What about identifying biased beliefs in defendants? Use of the reasonable person standard in assessing a defendant's actions is supposed to prevent biased beliefs from excusing the use of lethal force. It can be difficult to know for sure whether Hattori's race affected Peairs's belief that his life was in imminent danger. So, we focus instead on whether a reasonable person in Peairs's situation *could* have had such a belief.

With this question in mind, we need to ask questions such as: What were the grounds for a reasonable belief in imminent danger? Was there good evidence that Peairs faced imminent danger? Here's what the appeals court said:

> While we do not doubt that Rodney Peairs' fear of impending bodily harm was genuine, we nevertheless find nothing within the record to support his assertion that such fear was reasonable. Prior to the shooting, Yoshi and Webb had announced their presence by ringing the doorbell of the Peairs' home. Testifying that he believed Yoshi to be armed, Rodney Peairs conceded that he did not see a gun, a knife, a stick, or a club—only an object which he later ascertained to be a camera. In the well-lit carport, Rodney Peairs stated that he observed an oriental person proceeding towards him and that he appeared to be laughing. (*Hattori v. Peairs*, 5)

Peairs also had the evidence of Bonnie Peairs's earlier calling for him: "Get the gun!" Peairs testified that he had never seen his wife so frightened. Seeing her so frightened is surely some evidence of a serious threat. The appeals court took note of this fact and replied:

> The court believes very sincerely that a reasonable person would have responded with "Why do I need a gun? What did you see, Bonnie?"

The court is here noting the *availability* of evidence: Peairs could have made a quick inquiry and not just formed his belief based on evidence he currently had. A reasonable person would have made such an inquiry.

We see the appeals court here focused on both the goodness of Peairs's evidence and the availability of evidence, in judging that Peairs's belief about imminent danger was unreasonable. The court found not only that Peairs's grounds were insufficient for a belief that he was in imminent danger, but also found that Peairs failed to take in all the evidence in the situation as it unfolded over a few minutes. One bit of evidence was that Hattori and his friend rang the doorbell, announcing their presence; another bit of evidence was that Hattori was smiling and said, "We're here for the party." The court held this was all available evidence about whether Peairs faced an imminent threat, and he did not make use of it.

The requirement that one use all the available evidence is demanding. This requirement means it is no excuse to say, "I was blinded by fear, and that prevented me from taking in all the available evidence." Blinding fear cannot make a belief reasonable. Imagine saying, "My fear is reasonable, because it made me aware only of the possibility of being harmed and nothing else." A narrowed base of evidence owing to hyperfocus does not make your fear reasonable. Similarly, fear cannot make it reasonable to believe any less than all the available evidence.

Someone might object, "These criteria you are proposing for reasonable belief are too demanding. On less demanding criteria, Peairs's belief was reasonable." What weaker criteria might an objector have in mind? One might argue that a reasonable belief is just a rational belief, and then also claim that a rational belief is a belief that simply coheres with the evidence one currently has in one's possession. Many theorists advocate for this view about rational belief: so-called subjective Bayesians hold that one's belief is rational if it coheres with the evidence one has. Applied to Peairs's case one might argue this way: Peairs doesn't have to gather all the available evidence in his situation to have a rational belief. Given the evidence he did manage to take in—his wife's fear and panic—his belief was coherent and proportional to his evidence. And reasonable belief is just rational belief, so Peairs's belief is reasonable.[7]

In response to this line of thought, we might grant that rational belief doesn't require taking in all the available evidence in one's situation—it requires something less, namely, coherence with one's current evidence. But granting this puts a strain on the "rationality hypothesis" that reasonableness is just a matter of rationality. We expect people to take in salient and relevant information about their environment, and if they don't, then we do not think their beliefs are reasonable. Think about cases of dogmatic belief; it is common sense to say that dogmatic belief is unreasonable. A dogmatic person refuses to make use of available evidence. So reasonable belief goes beyond rational belief, understood in terms of coherence with one's currently possessed evidence.

There is a better way of arguing for the reasonableness of Peairs's belief that he was in imminent danger. One could argue that Peairs did take in all the available evidence, but he put a different construal on it, weighing certain factors more heavily than others. The basic idea here is that reasonable belief is permissive: If you present two people with the same evidence, it is possible for them to form different beliefs, both of which are reasonable.

Several facts motivate permissivism about reasonable belief. First, evidence is frequently messy: witnesses can disagree, some evidence points one way, some another. Our case illustrates the messiness of evidence: Hattori had a camera around his neck—did it look like a weapon? Maybe in some ways yes and in some ways no. Hattori was moving quickly—would that have seemed like evidence of aggression or not? Second, people can have different standards for what counts as good reasoning, or what counts as a good explanation: One person might think simpler explanations are more likely to be true, while another person might favor complex explanations that encompass every detail of a situation. Such virtues can compete against each other: Which is better, a plausible story about how all the evidence fits together or a single piece of highly damning evidence? These virtues can tug in opposite directions and reasonable people can value these virtues differently. Similarly, one must balance the risk of false negatives versus the risk of false positives, and people will differ in how they decide the question of which risk matters more. Moreover, there may be no straightforward way to adjudicate which of these competing epistemic values matters more.

It seems then that reasonable belief is permissive. In a given situation, there may be more than one reasonable response to the same evidence. Two people may differ in the beliefs they form, even though they make use of all the same evidence. This fact can explain how two jurors can hear the same evidence in a trial, and one reasonably believes the defendant guilty while the other reasonably believes the defendant not guilty.

The most compelling defense of the reasonableness of Peairs's belief appeals to permissivism about reasonable belief. One could argue that Peairs possessed all the available evidence, but he construed some of it as more important than other evidence, in a reasonable way, and differently than the judge in his civil trial. So Peairs might reply to the judge: *Yeah, they rang the doorbell, but why care so much about that? I cared more about the way he didn't stop when I said, 'Freeze!'*

The most compelling reply to this defense is to notice that there are limits on what counts as a reasonable belief, even if our notion of reasonable belief is permissive: Not just any response to the evidence is reasonable. This fact becomes important when we turn to the second component of Peairs's belief. Peairs's defense did not rest only on a belief about imminent danger. It also required the reasonableness of his belief that killing Hattori was necessary, that is, that there was no other way to save himself.

What was Peairs's evidence that there was no other way to save himself than to kill? Cynthia Lee raises questions about the moments before Peairs threw open the door to the carport: "Peairs did not have to go outside in the first place. He could have quickly locked the doors and called the police" (Lee 2003, 169). Let's focus on the moments after Peairs opened the carport door. He said "Freeze!" and Hattori kept moving toward him, coming around a car in the carport. This might have suggested to Peairs that he had to do something. The appeals court raised doubts about whether Hattori's movement toward Peairs was sufficient evidence for Peairs's belief that there was no other thing for him to do than to kill. The court said, "Rodney Peairs saw Yoshi at the back of the Toyota. He had sufficient time to shut the door, which Bonnie had done earlier." Likewise, in Peairs's civil trial for damages, the judge had asked him why he did not simply shut the door. Bonnie Peairs had done so moments before; why could he not have done so as well? Peairs replied that he had opened the door wider than Bonnie had. The appeals court reviewed this claim:

> The [earlier trial] court inquired as to why he did not shut the door. The excuse, well, the second time the door was open wider. So what? We know that when Rodney Peairs first saw Yoshi, he was further away than when Bonnie had seen him, and she was able to shut the door.

Here, it seems the trial judge's reasoning is not exactly to the point: It does not matter that *we* know Hattori was farther away than when Bonnie managed to shut the door. Peairs might not have known this. But it doesn't matter what we or Peairs knew on this score. Peairs did not need to know exactly how far away Hattori was when Bonnie managed to shut the door, or really to know anything at all about how she managed to do so. The point the court should have pressed was simply that Peairs could judge for himself that he had time to shut the door. In grounding this claim, the appeals court judged that a reasonable person in Peairs's situation would have had all the evidence he needed to believe that he could successfully shut the door before Hattori could pose any threat.

The court did not provide the details of their reasoning here, but we can expand on what their thinking might have been. The court reached a conclusion: "There was no justification whatsoever that a killing was necessary for Rodney Peairs to save himself and/or to protect his family." In other words, *no reasonable person* would think killing was necessary in Peairs's circumstances. Even if permissivism about reasonable belief is true, there are limits on what counts as a *reasonable belief*, or a reasonable construal of the evidence. To say there are limits is not to say there is a *single interpretation* that *any reasonable person would make of the situation*, but rather that some *interpretations* would be made by *no reasonable person*. In Peairs's case, no reasonable person would have thought that he could not shut the door in time. After all, Peairs had time enough to first identify where Hattori was, to track him as he approached from around a car, to shout "Freeze!", and wait to see whether he was still approaching, to take aim, and to fire a gun. This all happened quickly. But the question is, would this amount of time permit Peairs to close the door that he was standing in? Surely it had to be: All it would take was a simple step backward from the threshold, and a swift movement of the arm. No reasonable person would deny that Peairs could complete this action in less time than it took him to do what he did.

Reasonable belief is permissive—there is more than one reasonable way to respond to the evidence—but not just anything goes. There are some beliefs that no reasonable person would have, some interpretations of evidence that are beyond the pale. Witness Peairs's belief that it was necessary to kill.

There are many ways a belief can be unreasonable. That's because a reasonable belief has a lot of important epistemic qualities, and failing to have any one of them can earn your belief the status of being unreasonable. A reasonable belief is based on and proportional to all the available evidence, free of bias and dogmatism. At bottom, each of these qualities makes a belief more likely to be true, and truth is something we want in a belief. Reasonable belief is also a permissive notion: Two people can construe the evidence before them differently, owing to their background beliefs, their standards of evidence, and so on; consequently, reasonable people can form different yet entirely reasonable beliefs on the strength of the same evidence. Disagreements in our beliefs do not entail a failure on any one person's part to reasonably respond to the evidence. That said, there are limits on what counts as a reasonable disagreement. To admit a range of reasonable construals of the evidence is not to say, "anything goes."

The idea of reasonable differences in our beliefs, within reasonable limits, is a central idea in political life. To live together we need to navigate differences in our most firmly held beliefs. Knowing that some of these differences are reasonable is vital for living together.

8

Reasonableness in Political Life

We disagree about lots. We disagree about facts: Do masks prevent transmission of viruses? Does gentle parenting produce spoiled children? We disagree about how to act: Should you go vegan? Should you be allowed to "stand your ground" if you face a violent situation? We disagree about what makes for a good life: For some of us, the good life is about material possessions, for others it is about spiritual development, or relationships with friends and family.

Our disagreements can turn violent. For instance, in the last several years, the Department of Justice has charged dozens of people for separate attacks on abortion clinics around the country. The attacks involve vandalism, bomb threats, Molotov cocktails, and worse: In 2015, in Colorado Springs, Colorado, Robert Dear Jr. forced his way into a Planned Parenthood clinic and killed two people.

How can we manage to live together peacefully despite our disagreements? This is a fundamental political question. The philosopher John Rawls spent decades of his life thinking about this question. "We have a particular problem," Rawls told an interviewer. "How many religions are there in the United States? How are they going to get on together? One way, which has been the usual way historically, is to fight it out, as in France in the sixteenth century. That's a possibility. But how do you avoid that?" (Rawls 1998).

France in the sixteenth century saw Catholics pitted against Protestants in fighting that lasted more than three decades. Millions of people died, directly from the violence or indirectly from the resulting famine and disease. (It didn't help that during the French Wars of Religion, France was simultaneously fighting wars against England and Spain and the bubonic plague was sweeping through Europe. Sixteenth-century France might have been exciting for other reasons, but the political scene was not something to envy.)

An *illiberal* political system establishes order at the cost of individual freedom by, say, forcing everyone into a single state religion, or forcing everyone to abandon all religion. But the United States aims to be a liberal democracy. We want individual freedoms, such as religious freedom or "freedom of conscience," so that each person can pursue their own conception of the good life. And we want to live together as equals, each of us with a voice in political decisions and equal access to opportunities. These two things, freedom and equality, are aims of a liberal democracy ("liberal" not in the sense of left-leaning, but in the sense of emphasizing individual freedoms). Given that this is what we want, the central question for Rawls is how to get it and keep it.[1]

The challenge is that we are profoundly divided, not just by our religious convictions, but also by moral and philosophical doctrines. Some of us believe in the importance of community and think that social institutions should aim at fostering our sense of belonging; others emphasize individual rights and personal autonomy (communitarians versus libertarians). Some of us believe actions are morally right if they produce the greatest happiness for the greatest number of people; others believe actions are only right if we adhere to our moral or religious duties—actions that decidedly might *not* produce the greatest happiness for the greatest number (utilitarians versus deontologists).

Rawls notes that our religious, moral, and philosophical convictions come in bundles—our "worldviews" are packages of our fundamental convictions about human nature, our place in the universe, what is right and wrong, and what comprises a good life. Some of us believe humans have immortal souls, or that we possess free will, and some of us don't. Deep metaphysical views lead to further ideas about what is right and wrong, and about what we should ultimately aim at in living our lives. These ideas lead to further ideas about what's permissible in society, and on and on. One's whole worldview tends to hang together.

Profound difference in our worldviews is a fact of life. Rawls emphasizes that people who are reasonable and rational can come to different judgments about issues, even though they possess the same evidence and consider the same reasons. The resulting pluralism is not a disaster, Rawls says, "but rather . . . the natural outcome of the activities of human reason under enduring free institutions."[2] If we are free to think and act, we come up with different ideas about how to live, and that's a good thing. Rawls explains further why we can expect deep differences in reasonable worldviews. "Many of our more important judgments are made under conditions where it is not to be expected that conscientious persons with full powers of reason, even after free discussion, will all arrive at the same conclusion," he writes (2005, 58). Our education and life experiences vary, scientific evidence is complex and conflicting, we use vague concepts, and we weigh evidence differently.[3] In these and many other ways, people can be reasonable and rational yet find themselves with different packages of fundamental commitments.

Given human weakness, we can also expect some eccentric, intolerant, or outright wicked worldviews. Think of Gustavo "Gus" Fring, the fictional drug lord in *Breaking Bad,* who values people only for their usefulness to him; if anyone threatens his empire, he eliminates them without remorse. If too many of us were committed to intolerant or wicked worldviews there would be no chance of our living together in a liberal democracy. It would be game over. But in a more hopeful scenario, our society isn't filled with intolerant or wicked worldviews, and we stand a chance. So then, the question is, how can we have liberal democracy given a multiplicity of reasonable worldviews?

What makes a worldview reasonable? If we think a worldview is only reasonable if it is tolerant of other worldviews, then the answer to this question seems too easy. Of course we can have a liberal democracy if everyone is tolerant of everyone else's worldview. I suggest we should say instead that what makes a worldview reasonable is just that one forms it through living the life of a reasonable person—a good value-mapper, with all the dispositions and qualities we have been uncovering.[4]

Immense variety in otherwise reasonable worldviews creates a challenge for liberal democracy. Our deep moral and philosophical convictions underpin divergent understandings of what is just, and what our society should look like. But to live together under a liberal democratic arrangement, we need to agree on some basics. We need to agree on what Rawls calls "principles of justice," that is, fundamental principles governing how society will distribute the primary goods it produces: rights and liberties, income and wealth, access to opportunities for education and employment, and so on. But because we reasonably disagree in our worldviews, it seems we will not endorse the same principles of justice. And without agreement on principles of justice, there is little chance of agreement about how society's political, social, and economic institutions should look. Conflict in our worldviews seems to mean that the prospects for liberal democracy are dim. As Rawls told an interviewer, "I'm concerned about the survival of constitutional democracy. How can religious and secular doctrines of all kinds get on together and cooperate in running a just and effective government?" (Rawls 1998).

Rawls's goal is to say how liberal democracy might be possible, given the challenge posed by our differences. "How is it possible,"

Rawls asks, "for there to exist over time a just and stable society of free and equal citizens, who remain profoundly divided by reasonable religious, philosophical and moral doctrines?" (Rawls 2005, 4). It might seem that the answer is that it isn't possible. But Rawls was hopeful. Our capacity for reasonableness is the key.

The first step is to show it is possible, despite our differences, to reach agreement on basic principles of justice. Rawls offers a thought experiment as a proof of possibility. Start by imagining people tasked with designing the basic principles of justice around which to build their society. Suppose that these people are reasonable and rational, and that they believe in freedom and the political equality of all people. Next, imagine they face conditions of moderate scarcity, so they have an impetus to cooperate with each other. Finally, imagine that they are in the dark about the particulars of the life they will lead in the society that they design. They do not know what their individual characteristics will be, what their skills will be, or what conception of the good life they will have. They don't know whether they will be born into wealth or poverty, whether they will be especially talented, or what work they will enjoy. Imagine they are, Rawls says, behind a "veil of ignorance" as they deliberate about the basic principles of justice. Not knowing what their place in society will be, they will choose principles of justice carefully. The principles they choose will, after all, determine who gets what, and how they will fare. Behind a veil of ignorance—not knowing what their own role will be in the society for which they are hammering out a constitution—reasonable and rational people will agree to just principles, Rawls argues.[5]

Specifically, Rawls argues that reasonable and rational people will hit upon two principles. One is the principle of "greatest equal liberty," to the effect that each person should have an equal right to the most extensive total system of basic equal liberties. The other is a two-part principle governing how inequalities are distributed: a "Difference Principle" to the effect that whatever inequalities arise in our society should benefit the least advantaged, and a principle of "equal opportunity" to the effect that inequalities, say, in the size of paychecks, should only attach to positions that are open to all people, not just to people with a hereditary status (Rawls 1999, 266).

We won't go into Rawls's detailed arguments about why reasonable and rational people would hit upon the specific principles he identifies.[6] There is healthy, ongoing debate about whether he is right about which principles are just. What interests us is Rawls's reliance on the *reasonableness* of citizens in his story of how we might choose just principles, and how we might agree on a constitutional framework for a society. Why reasonableness? One might think that all Rawls needs to appeal to is people's rationality. Being rational, according to Rawls, involves having a conception of what counts as a good life and being able to take the most efficient means to realizing one's conception. From behind the veil of ignorance, it seems that a rational person might choose just principles because such principles will benefit them. They value their freedom, and they want to maximize it, and they want to be able to pursue their individual conception of the good life, whatever conception that turns out to be; not knowing what their actual position in society might be, they will want assurance that the social organization is favorable to the least well-off. After all, they might end up being one of the least well-off. But Rawls is adamant that it is our reasonableness that ensures we will choose just principles.

According to Rawls, what a reasonable person brings to the table, beyond rationality, is a willingness to enter into agreements with others, a willingness to propose fair terms of cooperation, and a willingness to stick by the agreements that they make (provided others do as well) simply because the agreements are fair. A reasonable person will not abandon an agreement out of self-interest. By requiring that the designers of the constitution be reasonable, Rawls believes, we ensure that the principles of justice chosen will be fair.

And being fair, these principles will both be appealing to individuals and stand a chance of gaining agreement.

Let's step back for a moment. Does Rawls rely on our ordinary understanding of reasonableness? Or is he introducing a technical notion when he talks about how reasonable people will choose? Here's why this question matters: If Rawls is using a technical notion, that would cast doubt on the idea that it is possible for *us* to achieve a liberal democracy. Who knows if we are reasonable in some technical sense of the term. Worse still, if by "reasonable" Rawls just means "someone who is committed above all to achieving and maintaining a liberal democracy," then he won't have proved anything by showing that "reasonable" people can achieve and maintain liberal democracy.

So, the question is, do we recognize in Rawls's reasonable person someone we would ourselves describe as reasonable? Is he talking about garden-variety reasonableness? Here is a way to test. Rawls gives the reasonable person a big job—namely, hammering out a constitutional framework that people with different worldviews can agree to because it is fair. Does it make sense to give a reasonable person this job? It is natural to say a reasonable person will propose fair terms and stick by them. If we look back at Grossmann's study, we frequently use "fair" to describe a reasonable person. Imagine someone making an unfair proposal—you wouldn't say they were reasonable in doing so.

Moreover, we now have an account of reasonableness, and we can say more about why a garden-variety reasonable person would be concerned about fair political principles. Recall our starting point: Our initial insight was that a reasonable person thinks about what they are doing from other people's point of view. They are open to the possibility that what matters to others does matter, and they are open to changes in their own point of view. They also use their judgment about the correctness or appropriateness of other people's concerns—they want to get it right about what really matters in any given situation. Sensible critical concern for others' interests and point of view is the hallmark of a reasonable person in social interactions. This is why being reasonable makes one concerned about the fairness of basic principles of our political system.

So, it makes sense to think that garden-variety reasonableness helps people do the job of hammering out a constitutional framework that stands a chance of adoption. Rawls does not need to invoke a technical notion of reasonableness. Garden-variety reasonableness will do.

Showing that a liberal democracy is possible is one thing. Showing how it might be stable over time is another. Rawls's second aim is to show it is also possible to sustain a liberal democracy despite the centrifugal force exerted by our conflicting worldviews. Our reasonableness again plays a crucial role, on his view. In his late work *Political Liberalism*, Rawls leans on two ideas—*reasonable worldviews* and *reasonable arguments*—to explain how liberal democracy can be stable over time.

Let's return to what makes a worldview reasonable. We have seen that reasonable beliefs are responsive to evidence (Chapter 7). Since our worldviews are comprised of our deeply held beliefs, reasonable worldviews are responsive to evidence too. As Rawls says, a reasonable worldview "is not necessarily fixed and unchanging . . . it tends to evolve slowly in the light of what, from its point of view it sees as good and sufficient reasons" (2005, 59). As with reasonable beliefs, reasonable worldviews are not dogmatic. Fundamentalist worldviews that refuse any change are unreasonable, according to Rawls. Suppose someone is an extreme literalist who accepts every word of the Bible, with its accounts of the creation of the world and of people living for centuries. Suppose the literalist resists change despite having evidence against their factual commitments. We have learned that humans don't live anywhere close to 969 years, as Methuselah is said to have done, but suppose the literalist rejects the biological facts. Such a person has a dogmatic worldview.

How might people with divergent yet reasonable worldviews all commit to liberal principles and stick by that commitment? Rawls suggests we might find what he calls "overlapping consensus." For example, consider this statement from the Second Vatican Council:

> This Vatican Council declares that the human person has a right to religious freedom. This freedom means that all men are to be immune from coercion on the part of individuals or of social groups and of any human power, in such wise that in matters religious no one is forced to act in a manner contrary to his own beliefs. Nor is anyone to be restrained from acting in accordance with his own beliefs, whether privately or publicly, whether alone or in association with others, within due limits. The council further declares that the right to religious freedom has its foundation in the very dignity of the human person, as this dignity is known through the revealed Word of God and by reason itself. This right of the human person to religious freedom is to be recognized in the constitutional law whereby society is governed and thus it is to become a civil right. (1965, Article 2)

The Roman Catholic Church here endorses a liberal principle of religious freedom. To that extent, the Catholic worldview is reasonable in its tolerant attitude to the practice of religions other than Catholicism (Wenar 2021).

A reasonable Islamic worldview and a reasonable Catholic worldview and a reasonable atheistic worldview could all agree that it is wrong to use political power to impose a religious doctrine on everyone. Rawls emphasizes that achieving an overlapping consensus requires only that everyone agree on the importance of religious liberty, not that everyone agree on the reasons for endorsing it. The Catholic Church's reason for endorsing religious liberty is the dignity of the human being as revealed by the Word of God.

This is not the reason a reasonable atheist has for endorsing religious liberty. Fortunately, agreement at the level of reasons isn't essential for the stability of our democracy. What matters is that we are all committed to the same basic constitutional principles.[7] Our individual commitment to these principles can spring from competing worldviews.

Rawls's hope is that if our worldviews are reasonable, then they will tend to overlap on some important basic principles such as the principle of religious liberty—and this agreement will in turn tend to keep democracy stable over time. Again, we see him counting on our reasonableness to help us live together in a stable democracy. Is he right to count on reasonableness this way? Our reasonableness plausibly increases the chances of consensus with others who have hugely different worldviews.[8] We seek consensus on liberal constitutional principles, even if we do not have the same reasons for supporting them. Here's why: A reasonable person understands the permissive nature of reasonable belief, and it is not a big stretch from there to understanding the permissive nature of reasonable worldviews. Being reasonable tends to make one seek liberal constitutional principles. Such principles provide the permission to differ in our worldviews. So Rawls is right to hope that reasonable people might achieve overlapping consensus among competing but reasonable worldviews.

This brings us to a last point about how reasonableness helps us live together. It concerns the way reasonable people argue with each other.

Say you are hammering out fundamental political principles concerning the basic structure of our society, for instance the articles of a constitution. Suppose you feel the force of Thomas Jefferson's remark, "It does me no injury for my neighbor to say there are twenty gods, or no god. It neither picks my pocket nor breaks my leg." So, you believe it would be good to have a principle enforcing the separation of church and state. As a reasonable person, you know that reasonable people disagree in their worldviews; you know this disagreement often owes to both the free exercise of human reason and the complexity of life's questions. Consequently, you have a fine appreciation for the sorts of contentious claims people tend to disagree about. So you steer around contentious claims, and you appeal only to premises any reasonable person could accept. This is what Rawls means when he says, "Understanding how to conduct oneself as a democratic citizen includes understanding an ideal of public reason" (2005, 218). Reasonable people recognize the importance of living up to this ideal: they do not argue from premises that they know other reasonable people will disagree with—at least not when they're arguing about the basic architecture of a shared democracy.[9]

For example, consider a right to assisted suicide. Suppose you believe that assisted suicide violates God's commandment, but you also know your friend, a reasonable person, wouldn't accept this as a reason to write into the Constitution a law that prohibits assisted suicide. Consequently, you will not use your belief about God's commandment as a premise in your argument for a law prohibiting assisted suicide. It's not that you give up your belief that assisted suicide is wrong. It's just that in the context of trying to reach agreement about how to live together as individuals pursuing their own view of the good life, you see that you should not appeal to certain claims, even though you wholeheartedly believe them. The call to restrain yourself, to not argue from premises you believe, might seem strange, but Rawls points out that we already accept restrictions on the whole truth: For instance, we exclude evidence from a courtroom if it is gained through an improper search, and we don't ask spouses to testify against each other.

In 1997, the U.S. Supreme Court was considering two cases concerning the right to physician-assisted suicide. The question was whether dying patients have the right to choose death over a life of pain and suffering. People with strong religious convictions rejected a right to physician-assisted suicide. Others were convinced that constitutional freedoms supported the right. The question Rawls asks is how people with such opposed viewpoints should reason together.

Rawls and a group of moral and political philosophers wrote an amicus brief for the Supreme Court on behalf of a right to physician-assisted suicide (published as a "Philosophers' Brief" in the *New York Review of Books,* March 27, 1997). Summarizing their argument, Rawls (1998) said, "We wanted the Court to decide the cases in terms of what we thought was a basic constitutional right. That's not a matter of religious right, one way or the other; it's a constitutional principle. It's said to be part of American liberties that you should be able to decide these fundamental questions [about how to live or die] as a free citizen." In appealing to the Constitution, Rawls and his coauthors held themselves to the ideal of reasoning from premises other reasonable people could accept.

In June of 1997 the Supreme Court unanimously rejected the idea that competent, terminally ill patients have a right to physician-assisted suicide. Rawls acknowledged that there were reasonable arguments for this decision, even though it conflicted with his own beliefs. One such argument, he suggested, "is that it would be very unwise for the Court to establish a right like this which is so controversial. The Court's decision would depend on a philosophical argument of constitutional law and allow a right that a lot of people would object to. This would be my candidate for a good political argument against my position." Rawls says the Court's argument meets his requirement of public reason—the argument does not depend on a particular moral or philosophical doctrine. It is a separate question whether the argument is good: "Public reason arguments can be good or bad just like other arguments," Rawls (1998) notes. "There are many arguments within public reason, and that's the thing to emphasize."

We can think of Rawls's recommendation about how to sustain a liberal democracy in terms of a procedure. If you want to defend a political position, construct a justification for it that you can expect other reasonable people will accept. Bear in mind that other reasonable people can be quite different from you. Steer around any premises that you can safely assume another reasonable person would not accept. If after this process you still have an argument in favor of your position, then you go public with it.[10]

What about deep disagreement? For example, suppose Eva and Finn disagree about the standards for belief. Eva's worldview is secular and she believes what science tells her, while Finn's worldview is fundamentalist and he believes what the Bible tells him. Imagine Eva and Finn agree that the Earth is warming; Eva believes the science and thinks global warming owes to human activity while Finn thinks global warming is God's work, not caused by human activity. Eva and Finn have a fundamental difference in their epistemic standards that produces this disagreement about what in fact causes global warming. They can't argue in a noncircular way for their standards, so neither one can convince the other to change. (If Eva tries to convince Finn that following science makes sense, she will rely on secular claims, and if Finn tries to convince Eva that believing the Bible makes sense, he will rely on religious claims.) So, Eva can't convince Finn to accept science as his epistemic standard and Finn can't convince Eva to use the Bible as her standard. Theirs is a deep disagreement. Some philosophers worry that deep disagreement is a threat to liberal democracy. If we can't agree about epistemic standards, then we can't agree about the facts. And in some cases, we can't convince others to change their worldviews or their epistemic standards, so what can we do?[11]

Rawls addresses this worry with his account of good public reasoning. When we reason with each other about political decisions, that requires accepting some basic epistemic standards that govern how to argue and what to count as evidence. In reasoning with each other, we should respect "plain truths now widely accepted, or available, to citizens generally," and these plain truths, Rawls says, include the uncontroversial conclusions of science.[12] The idea, explains Wenar (2021), is that "citizens should not justify their political decisions by appeal to divination, or to complex and disputed economic or psychological theories. Rather, publicly acceptable standards are those that rely on common sense, on facts generally known, and on the conclusions of science that are well established and not controversial."[13]

Permissivism about reasonable belief might allow that Finn's *worldview* is reasonable. But when he and Eva argue about what to do (whether to reduce activities with high carbon emissions, or instead to do nothing), their *arguments* must meet certain requirements to be reasonable. When the question is what to do (say, about global warming) and we must act together, then we must reach consensus on facts. So, Rawls says, we must argue in a reasonable way with each other. Finn doesn't have to give up his worldview, but in the public sphere he does have to give a reasonable argument in defense of his favored option (doing nothing to reduce emissions). And that means the premises of his argument must accord with basic epistemic standards.

"People can make arguments from the Bible if they want to. But I want them to see that they should also give arguments that all reasonable citizens might agree to," Rawls told an interviewer. Why should they so restrict themselves? Rawls responds: "What's the alternative? How are you going to get along in a constitutional regime with all these other views?"

Rawls counts on reasonable people to take on a difficult job, constructing arguments for political positions that others can appreciate no matter what their (reasonable) worldview is. Why think reasonable people are right for this job? Constructing good arguments requires one to anticipate where others might reasonably disagree. We have seen that garden-variety reasonableness involves understanding what matters to other people. This understanding gives a reasonable person insight into where people will likely disagree. To be really good at constructing arguments that use public reasons as premises, though, you need to do more than reliably anticipate where reasonable agreement and disagreement lies: you also need to identify reasons that other reasonable people might accept. How do we do that? In the next chapter, we will see more about the way a reasonable person manages to identify *generic reasons*—reasons that hold good across a wide range of individual worldviews.

Rawls aims to give us hope. He aims to show us that a stable liberal democracy is possible, not just as a distant imaginable utopia, but as reachable from where we are (with a bit of time and luck [2001, 37]), if only we can be reasonable. In this chapter I have spent a lot of time on Rawls's story about the possibility of a liberal democracy because his story relies so heavily on reasonableness. Engaging with Rawls's account of how we might live together in a liberal democracy, we discover some new things we might have only partially grasped about reasonableness. Whatever our political persuasion, and whatever we think of Rawls's particular claims about principles of justice, exploring his theory reveals the power of reasonableness to serve as a positive force that brings people to agreement, despite their deep differences. Liberal democracy needs lots of support, and Rawls invites hope that our reasonableness provides that support, by helping to keep our conflicting worldviews from tearing us apart.

9

A Role for Reasonableness in Morality

Here you are, struggling after your rowboat capsizes in an icy lake. A well-dressed stranger sees you from the shore. You shout "Help!" and wave to him, pointing to a lifesaver that hangs from a post nearby, but he does nothing. He is unwilling to get his shoes muddy. The stranger may not be breaking the law, but our ordinary moral judgment says his inaction is wrong. Moral philosopher Thomas Scanlon's answer for why it is wrong is that the stranger is being unreasonable. He couldn't justify his action to other reasonable people. Imagine that our actions are based on general principles that guide our behavior. The stranger's principle of action is something like, "Everyone can go about their business without helping someone whom they could easily help, if helping would be inconvenient." You are reasonable to reject this principle.[1]

Scanlon makes reasonableness the heart of morality. How does he understand reasonableness? We need to see how he understands morality.

The television series *The Good Place* (2016) features Scanlon's book, *What We Owe to Each Other.* Spoiler alert: The universe of *The Good Place* is out of kilter. There is an afterlife, but most everyone for the last few centuries has found themselves in the Bad Place, no matter what life they led on Earth. An enormous and tedious bureaucracy runs the universe, and it's not at all clear who might feel compelled to fix the problem with the eternal justice system. Chidi Anagonye, a philosophy professor whose whole life revolved around being moral, winds up in the Bad Place. His position seems absurd, not just because of where he winds up, but because his life's all-consuming question—"How do I do the right thing?"—can seem to have no meaning in the universe he lives in. Apparently, there is no omnipotent divinity issuing commands and deciding just rewards. There is some bureaucracy, but the CEO, if ever there was one, has left the scene.

It's easy to wonder what makes an action right or wrong in such a universe. This is also a familiar question in our own world. If we do not think being moral is about following God's commands, then what else could make an action right or wrong? One ready answer is Utilitarianism, the view that an action is right if it brings the greatest well-being to the greatest number of individuals. Utilitarianism nicely fits with a view of humans as members of the species *Homo economicus:* We posit a unit of account for well-being ("utiles" of pleasure, say), and then we resolve moral questions the way we calculate a restaurant check. Utilitarianism also has significant downsides. In Ursula Le Guin's story "The Ones Who Walk Away from Omelas" (spoilers again), Omelas is a beautiful city where everyone is happy, except for one pitiful child whose life of constant misery makes possible the city's continued pleasant existence. The arrangement makes for the greatest utility to the greatest number, but it is morally repellent.

Scanlon spent much of his distinguished career at Harvard University building an alternative to the utilitarian view. His alternative, *Contractualism,* focuses not on our aggregate well-being, but on the standpoint of individuals. The basic idea of Contractualism, Scanlon says, is that "when we're thinking about right and wrong, what we're thinking about is what conduct would be permitted by principles that I'd actually defend to other people, and that they would actually have reason to accept" (Scanlon, n.d.). The morality of your action depends on its being justifiable to others—or at least to reasonable others. The stranger's failure to pull you from the icy lake is morally wrong because he cannot justify his not helping. Any justification he might try to give would not satisfy a reasonable person.

Why exactly can't the stranger justify his action? If he says, "I just didn't want to do it," what is unreasonable about that? On Scanlon's view, when we call something reasonable or unreasonable, we typically presuppose a goal. For example, say I am bargaining with you to buy your used car, and I make a very low offer. What makes my offer unreasonably low is that we are bargaining, and bargaining presupposes a goal of reaching a price agreeable to both of us. If we did not have this shared goal, maybe I could name any figure I wanted, and it would not be unreasonable to do so. As Scanlon sees things (1998, 162), when we assess the morality of an action, we presuppose that we share a goal, namely, the goal of living together on terms of mutual respect (Let's call this "the overarching goal"). Scanlon argues that given this shared goal, the stranger's action is unreasonable.

Let's return to you, struggling in the icy lake. The stranger seems to be acting on something like this principle:

> Selfish Principle: You can go about your business without helping others in dire circumstances whom you could easily help, if helping would inconvenience you in any way.

You have good reason to reject the Selfish Principle. But it seems that the stranger has his own reasons to accept the Selfish Principle. So how does reasonableness help to decide who is right? Here's how. First, form an idea of the burdens that the Selfish Principle would impose on you and on people like you in situations like yours. Clearly, the burden the Selfish Principle imposes on you is significant—you are about to drown in the icy lake. This burden gives you excellent reason to object to the Selfish Principle. Others in similarly drastic circumstances have similar excellent reasons to object. But is your objection reasonable? To decide this, we also consider alternatives to the Selfish Principle. Something like the following would be an alternative:

> Rescue Principle: If you can prevent something very bad from happening to someone by making a slight or even moderate sacrifice, then it would be wrong not to do so.[2]

We then ask about the comparative burdens imposed on people by the Rescue Principle: are these burdens greater than the burdens imposed by the Selfish Principle? How would the Rescue Principle burden people? The principle forbids one from simply going about one's business, so that is a burden. Our overarching goal makes this comparison the way to answer questions about which principles are reasonable. Anyone who has the overarching goal in view will see that the comparative burdens imposed by the Selfish Principle are unreasonable (Scanlon 1998, 195). It is reasonable to reject the Selfish Principle, in much the way one would reject an absurdly low offer for one's used car.

Scanlon (1998, 218) points out that we need to make a fresh judgment about what is reasonable in each case life throws at us. There is no rulebook or algorithm that tells us how to decide which principles are reasonable and which are rejectable. As Scanlon says, there is no way to "reach a decision about whether a given principle could or could not reasonably be rejected simply by reasoning in a purely technical way, without appeals to intuitions about reasonableness" (242). Multiple values are often at stake in our actions, and each situation brings different values to light (245).

Contractualism faces serious objections. It demands a lot of us. For example: over time, the Rescue Principle could be quite demanding. Right now, people are starving, and you are spending money on coffee and devoting your free evenings to watching movies. Certainly, your burden in giving your money and time to the needy is less than the burden the needy face if you do not help them. Contractualists respond here in several ways. They remind us that many moral theories are demanding if taken at all seriously. They point out that burdens can take many forms, so you can complain about a principle if it thwarts your ability to cultivate personal relationships, or to pursue personal projects. If giving a lot of your energy, time, and resources to live according to the Rescue Principle would rob you of the chance to have your own projects, or maintain relationships with friends and family, then you could reasonably object to it.

You might wonder whether Contractualism is too demanding in other ways.[3] To justify one's actions, one needs to consider the people directly affected by them, and the burdens one imposes on them. How does one do this? Must the stranger think about your specific reasons for wanting to be rescued? The stranger doesn't know your specific reasons—he doesn't know about that karate competition you're looking forward to, or how much your dog needs you. To justify one's actions, one also needs to consider people indirectly affected by them. Since principles of action license the performance of similar actions, the people indirectly affected by one's action on any principle will be lots of people, possibly far away in space and time, with hugely different interests and concerns than the person one is directly affecting. How does one justify one's action to so many different people? Take our stranger again. In defending the Selfish Principle, he is committed to treating other people on other occasions in the same way (1998, 202–3). What does the stranger know about what matters to these other people? It seems that there are too many points of view to consider and too little knowledge about those points of view for the stranger to even begin justifying his action.

Scanlon's solution to the problem is this: The stranger can think about justifying his action in terms of *generic reasons*—reasons most anyone in your situation would have for wanting to be rescued. Most anyone drowning in an icy pond has the same reason to want to be rescued: they want to avoid death. Generic reasons do not depend on your personal preferences, characteristics, or aims. They are based on what people want "in virtue of their situation, characterized in general terms." To know about generic reasons, we only need "commonly available information about what people have reason to want" (204). So, we might say, the stranger's task is only to adopt a generic viewpoint on the situation and think about what any person in such a situation would have reason to want.

A generic viewpoint might be at odds with each individual's point of view or desires. As Scanlon notes, if one takes a generic viewpoint on the action, "a certain amount of how things look from another person's point of view, like a certain amount of how they look from my own, will be counted as bias" (Scanlon 1982, 138–39). From a generic point of view, how things look to each individual might be erroneous. Imagine you don't want to be rescued because your life seems pointless to you. The reasonable stranger nonetheless sees a generic reason to rescue you. His generic point of view filters out your individual preferences as well as his own.[4]

How do we improve our ability to identify generic reasons in any given situation? Scanlon doesn't answer this question, but we can think of a few ways. First, one can improve one's ability to identify generic reasons by improving one's ability to think about counterfactual situations. (What if the water weren't so very cold, or so very deep—what might a person have reason to want then?) One can also improve one's ability to feel empathy with others. Imagining being in another's shoes is often one's best means for identifying generic reasons.

Scanlon sees a reasonable person as able to do an enormously important job: deciding what is right and wrong. The task requires impartially comparing the burdens a candidate action places on individuals affected. This task is made easier by taking up a generic point of view on the action and identifying generic reasons for and against it. We can expect a reasonable person to handle this job.

Imagine the stranger by the icy lake is a reasonable person. He doesn't want mud on his shoes (cleanliness matters a lot to him). He may be ignorant of the particulars of your point of view, but he can take a generic viewpoint on his action and impartially compare burdens. He can think from a point of view that transcends his own interests and yours. A person concerned to map the landscape of value will also be concerned to map it from thirty thousand feet, if doing so is itself a valuable thing to do. Reflecting on what actually matters in a given situation—the central thing a reasonable person is concerned to do—is a way to identify generic reasons.

Contractualist thinking is a lot like the thinking required by the famous "Golden Rule"—do unto others as you would have them do unto you (Matt. 7:12). Contractualism asks you to take up a generic viewpoint and think about how anyone would want to be treated. The Golden Rule is open to the objection that it forbids too many things. Everyone would prefer certain things not to be done to them (Scanlon 1998, 170). The criminal can challenge the judge who is about to sentence him, "Well, how would you like to go to jail? Not very much, I expect!" So, the Golden Rule seems to forbid punishing wrongdoers. Does Contractualism have the same problem? No. The contractualist insists that one weigh the generic reasons of everyone affected by the principles behind one's actions. The victim of the crime has generic reasons not to want the perpetrator to escape punishment and can reasonably reject the criminal's suggested principle of action.

Why be moral? A theist facing this question has a ready answer: Because it is what God wants. Scanlon does not have this ready answer. Being moral requires your action be justifiable to reasonable others. Being moral can mean doing things that are counter to your immediate self-interest. So why do it? Why follow reasonable principles?

Here's a case that brings this question home. In 2016, actress Lori Loughlin and her husband, fashion designer Mossimo Giannulli, sought out William "Rick" Singer to facilitate their older daughter's admission to the University of Southern California as a purported crew recruit. In an August 2016 email, Singer told Loughlin and Giannulli that he would "create a coxswain profile." Giannulli emailed Singer a picture of his older daughter purporting to row on an ergometer for inclusion in the falsified profile. In exchange for helping his daughter fraudulently gain admission to USC, Giannulli agreed to make purported charitable contributions totaling $250,000 as a quid pro quo payment. Giannulli paid $50,000 to an account belonging to the USC athletics administrator and paid $200,000 to Singer's sham charity, Key Worldwide Foundation. Giannulli forwarded the invoice to his financial advisor with a note: "Good news my daughter is in USC . . . bad news is I had to work the system" (United States Attorney's Office 2020).

Loughlin and Giannulli were just two of several dozen parents rounded up in a sting operation, known as "Operation Varsity Blues," when Singer began cooperating with federal investigators. They were parents who prioritized what they thought was in their kids' best interest over doing the right thing. The right thing is to let your kids' authentic qualifications determine their success. Why should these parents do the right thing? That would entail their children possibly failing to get into a top-ranked university and missing the advantages this brings (social connections, recognition, top academic programming). Giannulli saw the "bad news" about his action as consisting in his having to "work the system," but he was willing to do so. What reason can Thomas Scanlon offer him to do the right thing, given the potential cost to his daughter?

Let's suppose the principle of Giannulli's action was something like *present fake credentials if it helps you gain a position you might not otherwise secure.* Giannulli's principle burdens some people: for instance, the student who did not get into USC who had genuine qualifications as a coxswain and who would have gained admission had Mossimo's daughter not taken the spot. For the kid with genuine qualifications, not getting a spot is a big burden on her. A better principle, one that no reasonable person would reject, would be something like *only submit authentic credentials when applying for competitive positions.* Given the overarching goal of living together on terms of mutual respect, the principle permitting fakery is unreasonable. Now, suppose we explain all this to Mossimo Giannulli. Suppose he says, "So what? My kid matters more to me."

The contractualist's first answer goes like this: Humans are special creatures. We are beings who set ends for ourselves and we are able to reason about how to get our ends met.[5] You set ends for yourself all the time—you want to become a veterinarian, or quit smoking—and you reason about how to achieve these things. Scanlon says, "Human beings are capable of assessing reason and justifications, and proper respect for their distinctive value involves treating them only in ways that they could, by proper exercise of this capacity, recognize as justifiable" (1998, 169). Contrast what it takes to respect a creature that cannot set ends for itself or reason about anything—a giant sequoia, say. Giant sequoias have value: they are living beings, beautiful and important parts of the ecosystem. One respects a giant sequoia by not carving one's name into it, or by seeking to preserve its habitat. One respects a human by showing a basic concern to act in a reasonable way toward them, making sure one can justify those of one's actions that affect them, or burden them in particular ways.[6]

"So what?" Giannulli might say. "All that stuff about respect is pretty abstract. My daughter's chances in life are much more concrete and important to me."[7] To respond to this challenge, a contractualist needs to show Giannulli how it makes his own life (and his daughter's) go better if he is moral. The contractualist needs to show Giannulli that if he respects others by acting reasonably, that does something for him.

Scanlon argues that living together on terms of mutual respect is good for us.[8] First of all, it brings us a special sort of joy. That is one reason to be reasonable and to seek to justify your actions to others.

Think about the choked line at the grocery and the way people take their turn getting out of the store. A basic concern for others has you showing some self-control, not jumping the line. The fundamental reason we act this way is out of mutual respect. There is a special sort of (admittedly mild) fulfillment one can take in respecting others this way, and having others respect one in turn.

Second, beyond the joy mutual respect brings us, Scanlon argues that being able to engage in mutually respectful ways is central to some of the most important human relationships. Friendship and loving relationships require mutual concern and respect. And mutual respect is promoted by acting on reasonable principles. Rational principles of action, by contrast, are not built to promote mutual respect. Recall the case of the landowner who controls most of the water in his county, from whom you request a minimum amount of water. The landowner can make it rational for you to accept whatever principle of distribution he decides on—he can threaten to cut off everyone's supply and never negotiate again unless you accept his principle of distribution. Under this threat everyone might be rational to agree to whatever the landowner decides—even the most meagre allotment. His principle for distributing water does not show respect for you or your interests. Giannulli's principle—something like *act to promote my kid's interests above everyone else's interests*—might be rational, but it is not reasonable. His principle fails to promote mutual respect, which is a key ingredient in his having important relationships with others.

We can flip this point around. If you cannot justify yourself to others, your life goes poorly. As Philip Pettit (2000, 231) writes, "we shrink from the gaze of another when we realize that it is impossible for us to justify our behavior to someone else." If we have reasonable grounds for our actions, and we can justify our actions to others, we can look people in the eye and live without shame. Many of us feel this has tremendous value. As Rick Singer said after the Varsity Blues scandal came to light, "I lost my ethical values and have so much regret. To be frank, I'm ashamed of myself. I have woken up every day feeling shame, remorse, and regret" (Levenson and Del Valle 2023). Who wants to live like that?

On Scanlon's view, the questions *why be moral* and *why be reasonable* are related. Reasons to be moral are reasons to be reasonable. We answer both questions by showing how important it is for us to live on terms of mutual respect.

According to the contractualist, being reasonable has an essential role in our moral life. Being moral does not mean following divine commands or toting up the units of pleasure and pain one's action produces in the aggregate; it means considering how one might justify one's actions to other reasonable people. When I engage with others, Scanlon says, "I have to ask, 'What reason do they have to object to what I'm doing, and what's my counter?' That's similar to the old Golden Rule, but it's just not what the person actually likes, or would enjoy. It's also: 'What reason do they really have, given how they would be affected, to object to what I'm doing?' And what reason do I have? . . . That's the kind of thinking that we should engage in and (it seems to me) we often do engage in, although I may be kidding myself" (Scanlon n.d.).

Even if we are not convinced that Contractualism is the correct theory of morality, we can learn a lot about reasonableness by thinking through the contractualist's account. Engaging with Scanlon's theory of moral right and wrong, we uncover features of reasonableness—features we can recognize to be true of ordinary garden-variety reasonableness. Reasonable people are good at transcending their own points of view and the point of view of others to occupy a more generic point of view. We have also seen how one reason for being reasonable is to promote mutual respect among people. There is great value in living on terms of mutual respect with others and a reasonable person appreciates this fact.

10

Polarized Belief

People disagree about lots. Is global warming caused by human activity or not? Does the open carry of firearms promote violence or deter it? It is natural to think we can reach agreement about these and other questions by looking at all the evidence. But sharing all the same evidence does not always produce shared belief. Looking at the same evidence sometimes drives people further apart. When our beliefs diverge more after sharing evidence, we say that people have "polarized beliefs." Polarization can happen even when no one is making errors or being irrational. Given what we have seen about the permissivism of reasonable belief, this fact is maybe not surprising.

Surprising or not, social scientists studying the phenomenon of polarized belief warn us of its disastrous consequences. They liken the situation of polarized believers to that of individuals trapped in the infamous "tragedy of the commons." Psychologist Keith Stanovich, in his 2021 book *The Bias that Divides Us*, writes:

> We cannot converge on the truth and yet every party in our collective is individually rational at the individual level. The tragedy of the [epistemic] commons is . . . the conundrum that results from a society full of people gaining utility from

> rationally processing evidence . . . but ultimately losing more than they gain. (2021a, 52)

Stanovich's talk of tragedy harkens back to the so-called tragedy of the commons: According to the lore, individual herdsman share a piece of grazing land, and each makes individually rational decisions to increase the number of cattle he keeps, but the collective effect of these individually rational decisions is to exhaust the common land, which is not in anyone's interest. In a parallel fashion, Stanovich and others suggest, a "tragedy of the epistemic commons" arises when individual believers share evidence, and each makes good use of that evidence in rational inferences, but the collective effect of these individually rational inferences is to drive people further apart in their beliefs; not converging on a shared belief, they fail to act in ways that promote the common welfare.[1]

Are we tragically doomed to develop ever more polarized beliefs and consequently fail when it comes to collective decision-making? On my view, no—not if we are reasonable. If we are reasonable, no tragic consequences await us, even if we experience polarization.

To see why, we first need to understand how the purported epistemic tragedy arises. How exactly can it happen that we are individually rational in making good inferences from shared evidence, but we end up poles apart in our beliefs?[2]

Here is Stanovich's (2021a, 41) nice case and explanation:

> Imagine that two chess players, Bobby and Boris, are facing off and they leave the chessboard in the middle of the game to take a break. And imagine, too, that you and I are two spectators who enter the room at that point, having not seen the beginning of the match. You think that Bobby is the better player by a clear margin, and I think that Boris is, also by a clear margin. We both look at the board and see that white has a substantial advantage. Given our prior beliefs about these

> players, you think that Bobby is more likely white, and I think that Boris is. If we both now update our prior probabilities of who will win the match, Bobby or Boris, and if we are perfect Bayesians, our posterior probabilities will now be even farther apart. We have brought different assumptions to the interpretation of the evidence (board positions for an incomplete match), and we show belief polarization even though neither of us has acted irrationally.

We can call this case *Chessboard*, for short.

In *Chessboard*, neither of us is making a mistake in our reasoning. Neither of us is being dogmatic, retaining a belief in the teeth of counterevidence, or missing some evidence altogether. We each just interpret the board differently, and each of us does so rationally. That is to say, we simply use our existing beliefs to evaluate the new evidence—the state of the chessboard—to arrive at a new belief about who will win the match. All this is good epistemic behavior.

Stanovich calls this use of one's existing beliefs to evaluate evidence "myside bias." The mechanism Stanovich calls "myside bias" has been known for a while; it is the mechanism of rational belief update. When Stanovich talks about us being "perfect Bayesians" what he means is that we form our beliefs about who will win the match by following Bayes's Theorem in our reasoning. The political scientist John Bullock explains: "Bayes's Theorem is increasingly used as a benchmark against which to judge the quality of citizens' thinking" (Bullock 2009). In the *Chessboard* case, you and I are reasoning as Bayes would want us to. The basic requirement of Bayes's Theorem is to update your beliefs by assimilating your new evidence without throwing away your old information—that is, using your existing beliefs to make sense of the new information. In *Chessboard*, we are both good Bayesians, making use of our initial beliefs (also known as "priors") to make sense of the new information we receive. The upshot of good reasoning need not be agreement.[3] Rational belief update, as judged by the gold standard of Bayesian belief update, can result in polarization.

Myside bias, so understood, is not irrational—it is not a bad habit. Philosopher Hilary Kornblith (1993, 105) points out that when we hold accurate beliefs, using them to help us evaluate new evidence delivers epistemic payoffs: "Allowing our background beliefs to influence our perception of the data when those background beliefs are true can only contribute to a better understanding of the world." So why does Stanovich call this way of evaluating evidence a *bias*, then? Psychologists use "bias" in two senses: One is neutral and just means a tendency or habit (for example, "I tend to sleep late on weekends"); the other is evaluative and means a failure to reason well or to gather information as one should. "Myside bias" is the name for a tendency or habit. Kornblith points out that myside bias can be a good habit.

There are lots of *irrational* ways we can end up poles apart. Contrast *Chessboard* with a case where we end up with polarized beliefs because one of us is just plain violating norms of belief formation. For example, the famous German geographer August Petermann was so firmly convinced of the "open polar sea" hypothesis that he refused to acknowledge evidence against it. Petermann believed that the ice pack in the Arctic thinned out at the North Pole, and he hypothesized that in the summer the Arctic Ocean would be navigable. As it happened, he got a lot of evidence against his hypothesis: In 1875, after a harrowing journey, two British ships ran into a solid sea of ice. Managing to escape its clutches, they returned with news of their discovery, but that did not change Petermann's mind.[4] Imagine you and Petermann have opposing beliefs on getting news from this first expedition, because you are ready to accept the defeat of the open polar sea hypothesis and Petermann is not. Your beliefs are poles apart. But yours is not a tragic situation to which you are doomed by your rationality. Quite the opposite: Your disagreement is resoluble through a better use of reasoning powers. Specifically,

Petermann's better use of his reasoning powers—he is the one who refuses to accept the evidence because he wants his open-sea hypothesis to be true.[5]

Scientists are not immune to irrationality, and distinct scientific communities with the same evidence available to them can find themselves locked in disagreement because of irrationality. Social epistemologist Cailin O'Connor (2023) notes that there are lots of causes for polarized belief within scientific communities: "There are multiple mechanisms whereby scientific polarization might arise, all of which are at least somewhat psychologically realistic. If scientists do not trust those with different beliefs, if they (like the rest of us) wish to conform with peers, if they engage in confirmation bias, if they are irrationally stubborn, or if they do some combination of these things, they, too, might fall into polarized camps." Again, this source of polarization—however damaging it might be—is not the tragic kind. Scientists whose polarized beliefs owe to irrationality can extract themselves from polarization by being more rational.

The supposedly tragic kind of polarization arises in cases where we end up with beliefs that are poles apart even though we are assessing the evidence rationally. Stanovich details numerous cases where experimenters present people with the same evidence and their beliefs go in opposite directions, even though they are not irrational, stubborn, desirous of conformity, lacking in trust, or in the grip of any other biasing mechanism. Here is one example. In an early study of polarized beliefs (Lord, Ross, and Lepper 1979), two groups of people—one group in favor of capital punishment, and one group opposed—were given mixed evidence about the efficacy of capital punishment in deterring crime. Both groups were shown one study that suggested capital punishment was a positive deterrent and another study that suggested it was no deterrent. People who were initially opposed to capital punishment regarded the positive-deterrence study as less convincing than the no-deterrence study. And people in favor of capital punishment regarded the no-deterrence study as less convincing than the positive-deterrence study. You might have expected that when presented with complex evidence that does not speak wholly in favor of a particular conclusion, people with different initial beliefs might come to moderate their views, moving closer toward each other's opinion. But no: This study, and others like it, found that people who start off with opposed beliefs just get more polarized, even though they are presented with the same facts. It is extremely easy to end up with polarized beliefs. All you need is to be faced with new evidence that is somewhat mixed or indefinite in what it supports and use your existing beliefs to assess it.

On this last point, it is worth adding that we do not always find ourselves on opposite sides of every issue when we start with different prior beliefs. In happy cases, the evidence piles up around us and becomes overwhelming, so that if we are rational, we do not end up with polarized beliefs but with shared beliefs. In these cases, the evidence cannot rationally yield opinions that disagree. For example, we currently have overwhelming evidence that human activity causes global warming; so, this issue is not one about which we can have rational polarized belief.[6] It takes some irrationality to produce disagreement in this case. Polarization in our rational beliefs happens when the evidence is messy or mixed, and when we use our prior beliefs to assess the evidence, we get different assessments.

If myside bias—using one's existing beliefs to evaluate the evidence—is a rational means of updating one's belief, and a good habit, then the resulting polarization among believers is to be expected. But the resulting divergence in our beliefs seems problematic to Stanovich and others. Polarization is bad—the lack of shared beliefs results in gridlock on important social and political questions: "There are severe costs associated with myside bias at the societal level. In the United States (and in many other Western nations), political parties and ideologies have become the equivalent of modern tribes," Stanovich writes (2021a, 125). Stanovich asks us how we can combat polarization. If no one needs to be making any rational mistake as they form their polarized beliefs, we can't try to inoculate ourselves against polarization by being more rational. This is what troubles Stanovich and others; it is what makes for the air of tragedy. What can we do?

One approach—call it the Enlightenment approach—focuses on what each of us as individuals might do to avoid having polarized beliefs. Another approach—call it the Social Engineering approach—focuses on avoiding polarized belief through a societal effort to manage our epistemic environment in ways designed to produce more shared beliefs.

Stanovich favors the Enlightenment approach. He recommends that we each avoid using our "worldview beliefs" to assess evidence. "Worldview beliefs" as he defines them are value-laden and acquired "largely as a function of our social learning within the valued groups to which we belong and our innate propensities to be attracted by certain types of ideas" (2021a, 94). Value-laden beliefs generate polarization, according to Stanovich, so we should limit ourselves, when assessing new evidence, to using only those of our beliefs that are based on evidence and free from value judgments. For example, imagine you get mixed evidence that capital punishment deters crime. You see some studies that show it has a positive deterrent effect and other studies that show it does not. You also hold the conviction that capital punishment is wrong (you are a devout Catholic and you've read Pope Francis's declaration on human dignity). Stanovich (2021b) counsels you to refrain from using this conviction when you assess the quality of the evidence provided by the pro-deterrence study: "I am not arguing that it is irrational to hold [worldview] convictions or to use them in forming [beliefs]. . . . I am just saying that it is wrong to project them"—that is, to use them to assess new evidence.

Stanovich's advice might seem good, but it runs into a couple of serious problems. For one thing, it's not so easy to distinguish value-laden beliefs from value-free beliefs. Our apparently ordinary empirical beliefs can be the product of our value judgments, and this fact can be hard to discern. Philosophers of science have worked to understand how value judgments affect scientific inquiry; many of them agree that values affect scientists' choice of research topic, experimental design, hypothesis formation, and even their observations. For example, Lisa Lloyd (2006) and Helen Longino (1990) show how certain male primatologists' interpretation of female primates' sexual behavior is influenced by their valuing reproduction, as opposed to alternative social goods. These primatologists' scientific observations were demonstrably influenced by their value judgments. If even scientific observations can be influenced by the observer's values, it is plausible that many of our ordinary empirical beliefs might also be influenced by our values; and it can be hard for us to recognize when this happens. A more pressing problem for Stanovich's suggestion is that even evidence-based, value-free prior beliefs (if such exist) can lead to polarized beliefs. Recall the *Chessboard* case described earlier: When you and I assess the state of the board, we do not draw on deep, value-laden convictions from our "worldview," but we nonetheless end up with polarized beliefs about who will win the chess match.

If we cannot always reduce polarization in our beliefs by making ourselves more rational, or by consciously limiting the use of our existing beliefs to a special class of value-free beliefs, what else might we do to limit the polarizing consequences of myside bias?

Defenders of the Social Engineering approach suggest a different fix: Clean up the epistemic environment and individual rational believers will be more likely to arrive at shared beliefs. The Social Engineering approach is becoming an increasingly popular line on various epistemic problems (Levy 2022; Gerken 2022). To see how the approach works, let's consider another source of polarized belief: fake news. The philosopher Regina Rini describes fake news as a story that "purports to describe events in the real world, by mimicking the conventions of traditional media reportage, yet is known by its creators to be significantly false and is transmitted with the two goals of being widely re-transmitted and of deceiving at least some of its audience" (Rini 2017). (Rini says "at least some" because the creators of clickbait fake news merely want people to click on the article, not necessarily believe it; yet it takes a few people to believe it to keep the fake news item alive.)

Here is a case: Pizzagate. In 2016 social media posts circulated the fake news that Hillary Clinton was part of a satanic cult that exploited children in the basement of the Comet Ping Pong pizza parlor in Washington, D.C. Edgar Welch believed the posts and drove from his home in North Carolina, armed with an AR-15 rifle, to investigate. Welch made a video recording of his journey, narrating to his two young daughters, "I can't let you grow up in a world that's so corrupt by evil without at least standing up for you and for other children just like you" (Miller 2021).

How could Welch get caught up by such a crazy idea? Rini argues that Welch is not unreasonable: Shared political affiliation can make it reasonable to believe fake news, and Welch was reasonably moved by reports from people who shared his political affiliation.

Let's look more closely at Rini's line of thought. First, Rini claims that partisanship rightly has a role when we assess the reliability of others' testimony. Your political affiliation is a sign of your value commitments. (A staunch Democrat is committed to the value of equal opportunity, say, while a staunch Republican supports deregulation. Knowing someone is a Democrat or a Republican, you can bet they have at least some of these value commitments.) And, Rini claims, if you and I agree on our value commitments, then that rightly establishes me in your eyes as a more reliable judge of political and moral issues than I would seem to you otherwise. The inverse also holds: If you and I do not agree on our value commitments, then you have reason to think I am getting it wrong about something fundamental, and so you have reason to think I am not an "epistemic peer"—not as good a judge—at least when it comes to political and moral matters. In that case, according to Rini, I am someone you can reasonably dismiss. Second, Rini maintains, descriptive facts (or purported descriptive facts) such as *there were children in the basement of the Comet Ping Pong* are relevant to political and moral matters. So, if you and I are epistemic peers about political and moral matters, you can also treat me as a peer about descriptive facts. Rini concludes: It is reasonable to use partisan affiliation to assess a person's testimony about descriptive claims. If Edgar Welch knew that he shared a party affiliation with Alex Jones, that gave him reason not to dismiss Jones's claims about Pizzagate, but rather to treat him as a good judge of the relevant facts. So, if Welch believed Jones's reports about the sex ring in the pizza parlor, Rini concludes, that was a reasonable belief.

Individuals like Welch are reasonable, according to Rini, so we cannot solve the problem of fake news by teaching individuals to be more reasonable in their consumption of purported news. The problem of fake news, she writes, "will not be solved by focusing on individual epistemic virtue. Rather, we must treat fake news as a tragedy of the epistemic commons, and its solution as a coordination problem" (2017, 44). For example, one feature of social media that produces a toxic epistemic environment is bad conventions about information sharing. Historically the social convention was that you were accountable for a story you published; but on social media sites, people retweet stories and say, "a retweet is not an endorsement." Ducking responsibility this way, as one simultaneously adds to the chorus of falsehoods, produces a dangerous forest of misinformation. So, Rini suggests, we need social-level interventions to help institute and enforce better information-sharing conventions. Rini suggests we might rely on social media platforms (Facebook, Instagram) to help enforce better conventions.

What to make of Rini's suggestions? First, let's consider her assessment of Edgar Welch. Rini herself acknowledges that her claim that Welch's belief is reasonable is "a surprising conclusion." I agree. It *is* incredible to say that he is being reasonable in believing as he did. We can pinpoint his errors. He was not making use of all the available evidence when he believed only one person's reports. He also failed to proportion his belief to the weight of evidence: extraordinary claims require more evidence, and Welch's evidence was scanty. We might forgive him for believing as he did—he was a trusting sort, his heart was in the right place—but that doesn't make his belief reasonable.

So that leads us to ask, how strong is Rini's argument that Welch was reasonable? We can spot a few problems. Rini claims it is reasonable to take disagreement about value commitments to mean that the other guy must be making a fundamental error. But we have seen the contrary: Two people can disagree, yet both have reasonable beliefs (Chapter 7); so there can be reasonable disagreement, especially about complex political and moral issues (Chapter 8). Rini's second premise is also dubious: You might trust your grandmother about lots of moral issues, but not trust her about all the factual matters related to those moral issues. Your grandmother is right that it's morally wrong to expose others to unnecessary danger, but she has no clue about the efficacy of face masks. Sharing moral or political views with someone is no reason to suppose they track the facts that are relevant to those views. So, Rini's claim that it is reasonable to use partisan affiliation as a guide to factual authority is not supported by a compelling argument.

What to make of Rini's Social Engineering approach to the problem of fake news? She is wrong about Welch's belief being reasonable, but she might be right that we should not focus on criticizing individuals' beliefs and rather focus on toxic elements in our epistemic environment. It is true that social media bends traditional rules for sharing information, sometimes to the point of breaking. Maybe we need social fixes for the problem of fake news and the polarized belief it produces.

Before we go down the Social Engineering path, however, we should ask some fundamental questions. Who decides how to clean up our epistemic environment? Which epistemic behaviors will be approved and which will be disapproved? Will the decisions about such questions be democratic? Which institutions can we trust to enforce the norms we (or others) decide on? Social media companies are run by individuals interested in making money, and they may or may not prioritize cleaning up the information environment. "Verified" user checkmarks may not carry any special value.

Some further questions: What ensures that engineered solutions are consonant with our individual epistemic norms? If the engineers' solutions are not acceptable to an individual, can the individual protest? Will there be sanctions? Compare the behavioral economists who want to "nudge" people toward good decisions, healthy lifestyles, or saving for retirement. These economists assume that people down deep want to be choosing as they are nudged to choose (Sugden 2017). This assumption can be questioned. In the epistemic setting, would social engineers try to play to our rational capacities, to get us to believe as our better epistemic selves would, or would they be content if there were ways to dupe us into shared beliefs, overriding our better epistemic judgments? Social engineers with the goal of reducing polarization could feed some of us fake news to reduce polarization. That's not the way we want to be forming our beliefs.

Finally, how would these social engineers conceive of us, the people for whom they are building epistemic environments? Would they assume we are merely rational—only capable of making good inferences—or would they have the good sense to also take account of our reasonableness? Recall Sam Bowles's (2016) criticism of *Homo economicus:* Bowles argues that when economists design incentives for people as if they were members of the species *Homo economicus,* without taking account of people's moral motivations, the result can be incentives that backfire, "crowding out" or even eroding our moral motivations. We are moral agents, Bowles reminds us, and our moral agency plays a role in our economic life.

I worry about a parallel mistake on the part of social engineers aiming to design our epistemic environment. Might they fail to take account of our reasonableness? If those making the social epistemic decisions were insensitive to the special qualities of reasonable belief, might they build epistemic environments that "crowd out" or even erode our reasonableness?

This is not an idle worry. In discussions of polarized belief, we see theorists assuming that we are merely rational (Bayesian) agents and not taking account of our reasonableness. Theorists do not take account of our reasonableness in the set-up of the so-called tragedy of epistemic commons. Recall the setup: Each of us is individually rational, updating our beliefs in good Bayesian fashion, while at the collective level, we fail to converge on beliefs; as a result, we fail to cooperate and act in ways that promote our common welfare. This so-called tragedy assumes that we are merely rational believers, each of us locked into our individual polarized view of things. The theorists who describe our situation as tragic never mention our reasonableness. So, we can expect if they were elevated to the role of social engineer, they would not design their solutions with our reasonableness in mind, either.

How might our reasonableness help us avoid the so-called tragedy of the epistemic commons? Here are two thoughts, both in the spirit of an Enlightenment approach to the problem.

Reasonable believers are likely to be what the psychologist Jonathan Baron (2023) calls "actively open-minded thinkers." Actively open-minded thinkers search for arguments on both sides of an issue. They don't neglect counterarguments against their own claims. Baron hypothesizes that this is because open-minded thinkers have beliefs about the nature of good thinking that guide them to look for reasons on various sides of an issue. Baron and others have produced empirical research showing that actively open-minded thinking can reduce polarization.[7] Encouraging people to use open-minded thinking would not eliminate the need to use one's existing beliefs to evaluate new evidence, of course. But it might reduce the tendency to stick with one's beliefs after discovering that other, equally reasonable people have different opinions. The idea is that disagreement in belief is to be expected, but disagreement needn't be intractable for open-minded people.

Second, the so-called tragedy of the epistemic commons assumes that polarization is bad—that it must lead to disastrous consequences when it comes to making collective decisions about law, policy, and general welfare. Is this true? John Rawls tells us to anticipate that reasonable people will have divergent beliefs about difficult moral and political questions. Our divergent beliefs can owe to differences in how we interpret the meaning of complex terms or concepts, differences in how we assess risk, and so on. We need not think people who disagree with us are unreasonable. Now having learned about myside bias, we can add to Rawls's list of causes for divergence the fact that people use their prior beliefs to assess evidence, when the evidence is messy or needs interpreting. This is just another reason among many to expect that reasonable people may disagree with each other. Rawls argues that we can nonetheless reason with each other, using public reason, to come to collective decisions.

Someone might object: "Polarization means we will not be able to use Rawls's method of public reason." For instance, imagine this case: Bernie offers this argument for universal healthcare in the US: Access to healthcare is a universal human need (everyone gets sick). Equality of opportunity to pursue one's goals is a hallmark of a just society; ensuring access to healthcare for everyone also has economic benefits, since early treatment reduces the severity of illness and saves money later, and people are more productive if they are healthy. Chip thinks Bernie's premises are disputable. Suppose Chip rejects Bernie's premise about the economic benefits of universal healthcare (Cancryn 2019).[8] Given what Chip has seen, he thinks this premise is not true—universal care will not reduce costs. Imagine that Bernie and Chip have polarized beliefs about this—they look at the same evidence and are driven farther apart. "If they can't even agree about the facts," the objector says, "how can they reason together to reach a policy decision?"

In response to this objection, we should note that if Bernie and Chip are reasonable people, their conversation and inquiry has just started.[9] There is a lot that reasonable people can do downstream from finding out that they have polarized beliefs. They can check if the disagreement owes to factual error. Has someone got false initial beliefs? If error is not the cause and the divergence in their beliefs is the result of rational cognition from good premises, then they can see if more information would help. If they probe further, they might discover a mountain of evidence that favors one conclusion over the other about the economic benefits of universal healthcare. And if Bernie and Chip are both reasonable that would resolve their dispute. If they gather more information and still see the issue in a polarized way, then if they are reasonable, they will take that in stride. Reasonable people recognize that polarization can happen without fault; so they do not think the other guy must be a jerk. Suppose they get to the point where there is no more evidence to acquire and Bernie and Chip simply see the proposition differently because of the way they weigh risks of error, or what have you. Then what? Supposing they are reasonable, they can see that their dispute is reasonable. They then face a practical question of what to do: There is a good argument for the premise, and for doing as Bernie says, and there is a good argument against the premise, and for doing as Chip says instead. Will Bernie and Chip freeze in the face of their two equally good arguments? They are reasonable, so this fact alone won't stop them in their tracks. They may seek yet another argument for their favored policy, bypassing the contentious proposition.

Polarization in our beliefs need not have disastrous consequences. The consequences depend on what we do with our polarized beliefs. There is a lot that reasonable people can do when they find themselves with polarized beliefs. Moreover, if we have polarized beliefs and we're reasonable people, that shows us something—it shows that the evidence supports different, competing hypotheses. If we are genuinely concerned to get it right about the issue at hand (as reasonable people are), then this will strike us as potentially valuable information. Our disagreements may push us to discover new hypotheses that make sense of our evidence.

Garrett Hardin, inventor of the "tragedy of the commons," was an ecologist and a vice-president of the American Eugenics Society. He believed that the combination of immigration and a welfare state created the conditions for Malthusian catastrophe. These tendentious ideas motivated Hardin's "tragedy of the commons." Eventually, researchers debunked the idea that sharing common resources inevitably produces disaster. Elinor Ostrom's research on shared access to resources, and how commons are not bound to fail, helped win her a Nobel Prize in economics in 2009. Ostrom's idea was that the "tragedy" was far from inevitable, contrary to what Hardin believed. She made careful economic arguments that demonstrated that if herders decided to cooperate by creating rules for managing the land and monitoring each other's use of it, they could avoid exhausting the shared resource.

Just as we should have our doubts about the so-called tragedy of the commons, we should also have our doubts about the so-called tragedy of the epistemic commons. It is true that we can all have access to the same information, and as individuals we can handle that information rationally yet arrive at polarized beliefs. But this fact is not tragic, nor need it lead to tragic consequences. Though we may fail to achieve consensus about facts, once we recognize that this can happen to otherwise reasonable people, we can engage in further inquiry, further argument, and compromise. We can expect polarization among rational believers. How we handle our polarization is what matters. If we're reasonable, we can handle it.

We may not be locked in a tragic situation, our rational epistemic practices leading us to a Malthusian-scale catastrophe, but that does not mean we are in a good place. We face other ordinary kinds of catastrophe: Many people are often thoroughly irrational and unreasonable. Many people do not know how to argue with each other in a constructive way. Worse still, being unreasonable can win one positive payoffs. We need to think about why unreasonableness flourishes.

11

The Past and Future of Reasonableness

Our polarization goes beyond our having polarized beliefs. Polarized affect is on the rise. In a recent survey, researchers found that "Democrats and Republicans both say that the other party's members are hypocritical, selfish, and closed-minded, and they are unwilling to socialize across party lines" (Iyengar et al. 2019). In contrast to issue polarization, which is simply a matter of disagreeing about policy, affective polarization is hostility or animosity towards members of other social groups. Affective polarization around political parties is growing in the United States. As Noam Gidron and his colleagues (2020) write, "Americans' dislike of partisan opponents has increased more rapidly since the mid-1990s than in most other Western publics."

An aversion to opposing partisans might make some sense if partisan identity served as a strong indicator of political ideas. But ideas alone do not drive us to separate ourselves into political sects. As political scientist Eli Finkel and colleagues (2020) note, "the causal connection between policy preferences and party loyalty has become warped, with partisans adjusting their policy preferences to align with their party identity. For example, a recent experiment demonstrated that Republicans exhibit a liberal attitude shift after exposure to a clip of President Donald Trump voicing a liberal policy position." (The same identity-based policy preferences can happen to Democrats—this tendency does not affect only one party.) Affective polarization—a dislike of political opponents driven by sectarian identity—is one instance of our unreasonableness. Adopting policy preferences out of loyalty, not for good reasons, that's another instance of unreasonableness.

Who benefits from our unreasonableness? An obvious answer is antidemocratic characters of all kinds—demagogues, fascists, and totalitarians, as well as simple grifters whose interests do not extend beyond self-promotion. Our unreasonableness works in numerous ways to help such characters dismantle our democratic institutions. If we're unreasonable, we're less likely to hold those in power accountable for their actions, and public accountability for honest, reliable, and competent exercise of power is essential for democracy. If we're unreasonable, we are manipulable. For example, recently many people were brought to doubt the results of what were in fact fair elections, despite a mountain of evidence. The result? An unreasonable loss of confidence in our democracy that only aids antidemocratic forces.

Sometimes it is reasonable to lack confidence in our systems. Can we be confident that our representatives represent us? After *Citizens United* allowed vast sums of wealth into elections, the answer seems to be no.[1] Or, to take another example: Angus King, an Independent senator from Maine, says, "When you have these one-party districts, the only election is in the primary, and the winner of the primary will be the one who is closer to the views of the narrowest base. You can't be moderate. . . . I have a friend who is a very conservative senator, and he faced a primary this year, and I said, 'Good Lord, man, what are they gonna charge you with?' And he said: 'Being reasonable'" (Warren 2014).

As I write, unreasonable people have a great deal of power. Antidemocratic forces with shocking amounts of money are shaping our regulations and laws, influencing our elections and elected officials, buying news outlets and promoting unreasonable opinions. The people we elect increasingly cannot afford to be reasonable. Wherever you are on the political spectrum, you can be worried about the health of our democracy. How to effect the political changes necessary to strengthen and defend liberal democracy—this is a tough question in our current ecosystem.

With plenty of reasons to be pessimistic about liberal democracy's prospects, it can feel absurd to focus on our reasonableness. However, I am not suggesting that our individual reasonableness will cure our sectarianism, or by itself save our democracy. What I am suggesting is akin to what John Stuart Mill says in defense of free speech. Mill writes:

> I acknowledge that the tendency of all opinions to become sectarian is not cured by the freest discussion, but is often heightened and exacerbated thereby; the truth which ought to have been, but was not, seen, being rejected all the more violently because proclaimed by persons regarded as opponents. But it is not on the impassioned partisan, it is on the calmer and more disinterested bystander, that this collision of opinions works its salutary effect. (2011, 97)

Some have read Mill as believing that free speech produces a "marketplace of ideas" (in the words of Oliver Wendell Holmes) from which the best ideas—that is, the true ones—naturally emerge victorious. But Mill does not advocate the marketplace metaphor (Gordon 1997). What he says is less optimistic. Mill believes that free speech does not guarantee the truth will come out on top—it's more a matter of the truth having little chance without it.[2] In a similar vein, I don't suggest that individual reasonableness all by itself can cure sectarianism or secure our liberal democracy. It's more a matter of liberal democracy standing little chance without it.

Our individual reasonableness may not be sufficient, but it is necessary. And despite the power of the forces of unreasonableness, we can find reasons for some optimism. There are things we can do. For one, we can cultivate reasonableness in ourselves and others. We can talk about being reasonable, about what it means, and why it is valuable. We can teach children about the importance of being reasonable, in personal life and in politics. We already teach critical thinking skills and basic civics—we can also teach the notion of reasonable disagreement, and what is required for reasonable belief and reasonable emotion.

We can work to make our public discourse more reasonable. I acknowledge that appeals to "be reasonable!" may move only the "calmer and more disinterested bystander," not the "impassioned partisan." But I also believe we can be impassioned and reasonable at the same time. Our emotions can be reasonable. Consequently, they can contribute to public life. While a demagogue plays on people's emotions to whip up dislike of members of the other party, and a fascist encourages his partisan followers to feel disgust at others, it is also possible for reasonable citizens to make legitimate appeals to emotion in political life. Emotional appeals are an aid not just to successful election campaigns but also to successful laws and policies.[3] We can work to make our emotional appeals more reasonable, in something like the way we try to make our arguments more reasonable.

Rawls's ideal of "public reason," recall, is that we should give arguments using premises that all reasonable citizens might agree to (at least when we argue over constitutional essentials and questions of basic justice—who gets to vote, who gets to own property, and so on). Emotions can also have a role in public reason.[4] Imagine someone has vandalized your car. You are angry and you have reason to be. You can share your reasons with me, and even if I do not experience the anger that you do (maybe I can only muster some small indignation—I am tired, and there are so many cases of vandalism in the neighborhood) I can recognize your anger arises with good reason. We enjoy overlapping consensus in our evaluation of the situation, even though we do not share the same emotion. Our differing emotions can serve as grounds for shared public action.

We can even expect there will be cases where we agree in our reactive emotions—perhaps even in our moral disgust. A good example: We might all see reason for moral disgust at cruelty (Kahan 1999). Disgust at cruelty against animals is widespread in our society. It may be that the reason we each feel disgust is itself widely shared: Cruelty involves being indifferent in causing pain to a sentient being, and most anyone can see that nothing justifies that. Even if people do not share the same reason for their moral disgust, they might arrive at overlapping consensus on the disgust itself. For example, the Jewish tradition forbids cruelty to animals explicitly: no causing pain to any living creatures. Jains might agree, but for distinct reasons, non-violence being the primary reason. Both might feel moral disgust at cruelty.[5]

As we cultivate our reasonableness, we raise the likelihood that we can use our emotions to track value cooperatively. If we're reasonable, we can harness the power of our emotions when we deliberate together about what matters. Restricting our appeals to reasonable emotions, we will go a long way toward living in accord with Rawls's ideal of public reason.[6] The more we cultivate our reasonableness, the more habitable our public spaces become, and the more positive effect our calls to be reasonable can have.

So there are things we can do to cultivate our individual reasonableness and the reasonableness of our public discourse. But how ready are we to do so? More of us are ready than one might think. Many people feel unhappy with our sectarian political environment. Finkel writes, "substantial swaths of American society (including many who identify as Democrat or Republican) are fed up with surging sectarianism" (Finkel et al. 2020, 5). Although researchers have found that members of the "Exhausted Majority feel 'pessimistic' about the state of America's politics (72 percent)," a majority of people still believe "our differences are not too big for us to work together: 77 percent of Americans believe our differences are not so great that we cannot come together" (Hawkins et.al. 2018). One can take some encouragement here. Many people are repulsed by sectarian politics and crave a more reasonable public sphere.

As for our readiness to be reasonable, it also cheers me to think about the depth of this trait in human nature. Its roots are deep in us, in our development as a species. Here is a little "state-of-nature" story about how reasonableness came to be important to human beings. It's a story that invites us to imagine humans living before complex social institutions or governments, with only rudimentary forms of communication and cooperation. The plot of the story is simple: Humans in this primitive state face a very general need and they hit upon a way to get that need met. Here's the story in more detail.

Imagine these humans navigate their physical environment, mapping the physical geography, and they register value and disvalue, too—*nutritious* foodstuffs, *dangerous* predators, *useful* plants, and so on. They have the need to learn about value and disvalue in their environment, beyond their immediate location. Others might provide this information, but because each person maps value in relation to their own perspective, a potential lack of alignment among value-mappers creates the need for people to map value in a way that others find useful. This need is met when people develop the capacity to think about value from a point of view that is not their own. Add to this capacity further dispositions to create and sustain reliable and sharable maps of value—for instance, dispositions to take correction from others and to acknowledge ever wider circles of others with whom one might share judgments about value—and the result is people who are highly adept, impartial value-mappers. Such people solve the problem of sharing information about value and so effectively meet their need to know where the good, worthwhile, nasty, and harmful stuff is. They acquire a multifaceted trait—reasonableness—that bundles together the capacity to think about value from another's point of view as well as dispositions to create and sustain accurate maps of the value landscape that are sharable with other reasonable people. They come to use the word "reasonable" to mark adept value-mappers, to talk about who has accurate and sharable maps of value.

This little story is not meant as an actual history of how humans became reasonable or came to use the word "reasonable" to identify an especially useful sort of person. The story is timeless, or outside of time. But the depth and generality of our need to track value together suggest that reasonableness has a long history in our species. As long as we have managed to live cooperatively, we have met this pressing need by being reasonable.

Michael Tomasello (2022) tells his own story of two early humans hunting an antelope, one in the role of chaser and the other in the role of spearer. Each has to understand the other's role and their perspective on the hunt. My little state-of-nature story gains plausibility from Tomasello's story. The two hunters each must see the value landscape in a cooperative way. To succeed, both need to see the disvalue of losing the antelope across the stream and the value of a box canyon to block its escape. Tomasello focuses our attention on how early humans took on the risks of collaborating and managed to coordinate with each other on shared goals such as hunting large game. He argues that collaboration required "new forms of perspective taking and cooperative communication." I add that truly useful perspective taking must also include perspectives on the value landscape. I also emphasize that the desire to accurately understand that landscape shapes our perspectives into something worth sharing.

Anyone can tell a "just-so story" to explain the current state of things. But Tomasello's story is not a just-so story—it is backed up by evidence about human development from comparative psychology and animal studies. What backs up my state-of-nature story? It gains empirical support from Tomasello's own account because its story about reasonableness fits well into his account of perspective-taking and cooperation. Further, my story is also backed up by the way it explains our current appeals to reasonableness in our everyday life, in political and moral theories, and in the law. Over the course of this book, we have looked at a wide range of important uses of the notion of reasonableness, in ordinary life, in law, and in theories of morality and liberal democracy. We have seen how the trait identified in my state-of-nature story explains our practices in each of these settings. Successful explanation makes my little story a plausible one about the nature of reasonableness.

Tomasello goes on to argue that early humans' collaborations forced them to develop language skills, first pointing and gesturing, and then later language for protesting if partners defected from a joint plan. Tomasello's evidence is partly from comparative developmental psychology. As an example, he notes the following: "When three-year-old children have made a joint commitment to collaborate, and their partner does not play her role in the ideal way, they protest to her (which they do not do if she is ignorant of how to behave in this role). Children also protest if their partner to a joint commitment just up and leaves without an excuse or apology" (2022, 99). If early humans would have protested when others departed from a collaborative venture, might they not also have protested when others failed to see what was relevant or of value from their partner's perspective? They would have wanted a word to use in protest when a partner failed to track something important. Likewise, they would have wanted a word to express approval of partners who excelled at perspective taking and who were reliable in tracking what mattered. A word for *reasonableness* would allow them to flag partners who were good to work with. Who knows how long we have been talking about being reasonable?

Tomasello's story of our evolving capacities for collaboration is in part a history of our reasonableness. We bring a range of capacities to bear in our effort to see the value landscape accurately and cooperatively. We bring critical open-mindedness to bear as we see what matters to others; we discipline our value judgments with the goal of sharing information about value; we are also disposed to regulate our emotions with the goals of both accuracy about value and coherence with the emotions of other reasonable people; and we're inclined to discipline our beliefs by using all the available evidence and avoiding bias and dogmatism, with the goal of forming accurate and sharable beliefs. We are also inclined to discipline each other over failures to be reasonable, which serves to make us better at cooperatively mapping the value landscape. These are highly evolved capacities. It is natural to suppose that from early in our history, evolution has been building us to be reasonable.

Our species-specific skills for collaboration affect our experience of ourselves. As Tomasello writes, humans evolved to occupy a unique "experiential niche":

> Reptiles come to experience situations of obstacle and opportunity; mammals come to consciously experience their own operational level of functioning; and great apes come to experience their own executive decision-making and cognitive control . . . Early humans came to live in a social / cooperative experiential niche, structured by the shared worlds and recursive perspectives created by collaboration. (2022, 104)

We humans experience and enjoy our rational cognition and our executive decision-making, like any great ape. We also experience ourselves as reasonable. We enjoy uniquely human experiences when we exercise our highly evolved capacities for being reasonable.

Admittedly, it doesn't always feel great to be reasonable. It can feel great when you share the concern that people get it right about value with someone else. But what about when someone is wrong about what matters, and keeps insisting they're right? Then being concerned that they get it right can be maddening—a source of serious anxiety, even, when the person in question matters a lot to you. How does it feel to listen to others, to accord them some authority about what is worthwhile? Sometimes it is arduous. When we exercise the emotional, cognitive, and social capacities that make us reasonable, it doesn't always feel great.

That said, the uniquely human experience of being reasonable can be fulfilling. Each time we see eye to eye, get on the same page after a discussion, reach a compromise, or temper our emotions, we feel a satisfaction that is important in its own way. Getting it right about what matters, caring about others' perspectives on what's valuable, helping others steer toward the good things and away from the bad things—engaging in these human endeavors is a special experience.

My aim has been to encourage us to think concertedly about what it means to be reasonable. I am not suggesting that merely reflecting on being reasonable will make us more reasonable or deliver a cure for sectarianism. Optimistically, I believe if we think concertedly about what it means to be reasonable, that can help us grow our reasonableness and manifest it more regularly.

The history of political and moral theory and of legal systems shows our evolving reliance on reasonableness as a standard of behavior. These theories and systems make explicit appeal to one of our most powerful human traits—being concerned to see the value landscape accurately and cooperatively—a trait that has helped us live together successfully for eons. The actual history of humankind's reliance on the coordinating power of reasonableness is a history waiting to be told. So too has a comprehensive investigation into reasonableness through behavioral and social sciences yet to begin. I would be pleased if my study stimulates others to make their own studies of reasonableness. I would be especially happy if others disagreed with me about what it means to be reasonable. Disagreement would mean that more of us were thinking together about being reasonable.

Notes

Introduction

1. This brief overview of the case is based on the accounts in Lee (2003) and Forell (2010).

2. For clarity, I replace Forell's (2010, 1428) "mistake" with "mistaken belief."

3. Nussbaum (2004b, 36) writes, ". . . we typically think that people are reasonable if they accept the standard norms of their society. At any rate, as we shall see, the law typically thinks this, routinely equating the 'reasonable man' with the 'average' or 'ordinary' man." But Nussbaum also enters this caution: "Though the law tends to operate with the fiction that the 'reasonable man' is more or less the same as the 'average man,' . . . it is important for thinkers about law to go behind this assumption and to question it. The average man, being also a human being, exhibits a lot of tension, ambivalence, and, in normative terms, unreasonableness."

4. The jury in the criminal trial found Rodney Peairs not guilty, holding that he reasonably believed that his life was in danger and the only way to save himself was to kill. But in a subsequent civil trial, the judge found in favor of Yoshi's parents, holding that Peairs's belief was unreasonable. The difference in outcomes needn't be evidence of subjectivity in the notion of reasonableness, however, because criminal and civil trials employ different standards of proof—"proof beyond reasonable doubt" versus "proof on the balance of probabilities"—and this difference may be all it takes to account for divergent legal judgments about the reasonableness of Peairs's belief.

5. As John Rawls (1999) argues. Exactly how reasonableness makes democracy possible is a central topic in political philosophy. We'll see more about Rawls's view in Chapter 8.

6. If the case is different, our judgment about the owner's reasonableness differs. For instance, suppose the owner started his business without thinking about how to care for his employees if they should be injured, so he was unreasonable then, but now he is taking into account all the competing values in his situation. He knows that violating the law and handing the cost of care over to the public are very bad things. But he also knows how much it matters to his employees that he stays in business, and how much it matters to get his employees care if they should need it. He simply can't afford insurance. He intends to take the risk of filing a false police report, not his employee. He thinks hard about how all these competing values weigh against each other. In this case, one might argue, he is doing a good job of taking into account the competing values in the situation, and he's reasonable.

7. Pinker's (2021, 36) statement captures a popular conception of practical rationality. Rationality so understood takes for granted that agents have a goal, and so rationality does not include reasoning about what our goals should be. For a contrasting view, see Kolnai (1961). I won't aim to settle on a particular definition of rationality in this text. I will contrast reasonableness with various proposed definitions.

1. Being Reasonable and Being Rational

1. In a similar vein, Krugman (2007) says, "You might ask, why not represent people the way they really are? The answer is that abstraction, strategic simplification, is the only way we can impose some intellectual order on the complexity of economic life."

2. Quoted in Gardner (2019b, 274).

3. Gardner (2019a) has many head-clearing things to say about the reasonable person standard. I think the label "the reasonable person standard" invites confusion. We mean to refer to *the standard* that invokes *a reasonable person* (as opposed to, say, the standard that invokes a prudent person, or the standard that invokes an informed person, and so on). Instead, the label invites thoughts of *a standard* that invokes *the reasonable person.* From there we imagine a figure that embodies all forms of reasonableness at once, a paragon of reasonableness.

4. To get Scanlon's answer, we need to also assume that the landowner's sharing a minimal amount of water would not endanger everyone, leaving no one with enough water for his crops or for basic human needs.

5. Note that Gardner and Macklem's account of rationality competes with Pinker's definition, which emphasizes the inferential relation between one's beliefs and goals. Whose account is right? I won't hazard an answer. Adjudicating what it means to be rational would be a task for a different book. My aim is not to settle a dispute about which account of rationality is correct, but to draw the contrast between reasonableness and rationality, variously understood.

2. *Reasonableness in the Law*

1. Vagueness in the law is to be avoided: laws need to give people fair notice of what behaviors are punishable, and they only give fair notice if they are stated clearly and make definite prohibitions. Vague statements fail to give fair notice.

2. Because the law depends on us understanding what it means to be reasonable, the notion of reasonableness in the reasonable person standard must be the ordinary meaning of "reasonable," not a theory-bound notion. Legal theorists who approach the question of what the reasonable person standard *should* mean if it is to play a role in a legal system aimed at particular political goods, such as equality or freedom, pursue a different task than mine.

3. Mayo Moran (2003) is concerned about the law's use of the reasonable person standard, given the demand that the law treat everyone equally. What of those people whose individual characteristics make it difficult or impossible to "rise to their neighbor's standard"? Moran suggests instead that the core demand made by the reasonable person standard for the purposes of tort law is that a reasonable person is not indifferent to the welfare of others. A person who harms others out of indifference fails to be reasonable. (See especially her chapter 7.) On my view, indifference to others might make for unreasonable behavior, but lack of indifference—that is, showing some concern for others—is not the whole of what it means to be reasonable. How would indifference affect the reasonableness of a belief, for instance?

4. The following exposition is drawn from Whitman (2016) and Shapiro (1991).

5. As Shapiro (1991) explains, these theories of evidence were provided by both theologians working in the casuistical tradition and philosophers working with new tools of probabilistic reasoning.

6. This section owes a great debt to Waldron (2023).

7. For ease of exposition, I write as though juries do most of the fact-finding and verdict-giving, but in contemporary law, lots of decisions are made not by juries, but by judges or administrative review boards.

8. When Holmes wrote his classic *The Common Law,* he was familiar with a history of legal thinking that appealed to various personified standards of action. In *Vaughan v. Menlove,* the personified standard was "the ordinary man of prudence," not the "reasonable person."

3. *Reasonableness in Person*

1. The objector might try one last line of defense of Karl by arguing that Ann gave *implied consent* through her inaction. Setting aside that this is an awkwardly legalistic approach to a personal relationship, the idea is roughly this: "Ann's consent is implied when she fails to object in a situation where a reasonable person would object; a reasonable person could certainly object to Karl's taking the flight lesson with them in the backseat. Since Ann did not object, Karl is reasonable to carry on with his lesson." In response to this line of thought, to persist in its legalistic vein, we can say: Ann was likely frozen with fear and unable to object. This fact blocks the inference from her inaction to her consent. (In cases involving consent in sexual activity, being asleep, intoxicated, or fearful are all conditions that need to be taken into account in determining consent.)

4. *Mapping the Landscape of Value*

1. Is value an inherent property of a thing, or a response-dependent property, only present because one thinks the thing valuable? Our concept of reasonableness may be explained without taking a stand on questions about the metaphysics of value. For ease of exposition, I will often write as if many kinds of value are real, objective, or mind-independent: the value exists, independently of our thoughts about it. If a realist metaphysics of value is incorrect, our commonsense notion of reasonableness can take that in stride.

2. We can apply this account of what it means to have something matter to you to the case of being reasonable. I've said that being reasonable means

being *concerned* to get it right about value. This means that, if you're reasonable then *it matters to you* to get it right about value: you're emotionally engaged by the goal of accurately tracking value. You care to track value, and you are emotionally engaged by this goal. That is why if you are reasonable, you have the motivation to admit you are wrong.

3. Being justified requires having what are in fact good reasons and grasping those reasons. See Alston (1988). Another mistake one can make: Something can be valuable, and you can believe it to be valuable, but not for the reasons you think. Alter the story above with this one detail: Unbeknownst to you the watch your grandmother arranged as a substitute is a rare vintage piece with great monetary value. As before, the thing's mattering to you rests on good reasons, and it is valuable, but you are wrong about why its valuable. You can also get it wrong about what matters to you because you are self-deceived about your emotional engagement. The possibilities of error are many, but they do not preclude having good reasons for your beliefs about what is valuable.

4. Contrary to Gardner and Macklem's (2004) view, one needn't have undefeated reasons to be reasonable.

5. American appeals court judge Learned Hand thought we might replace judgments of negligence with an expected utility calculation, weighing up probabilities of losses and benefits, and the costs of avoiding or achieving each. See United States v. Carroll Towing Co., 159 F.2d 169 (2d Cir. 1947). But Hand's idea is beset with the difficulties of assigning numeric values to outcomes. In some cases, we might rightly object to assigning a numeric value to things: Does a human life matter more than the cost of equipping cars with safety features—what numeric value do we assign to human life?

6. A defender of the first explanation might say there is value (worth, goodness) in the quiet moment, but *valuing* it does not make sense in the captain's situation. His emotional engagement in this option is lacking.

7. Our capacity for deliberating about what to do is called "practical reason" by philosophers. Wallace (2024) suggests this capacity requires us to be value-mappers. I am suggesting that being reasonable is being good at value-mapping. So, if Wallace is right, then practical reason requires reasonableness.

8. You might say a map of value is by its nature sharable—it's a map of value after all, and anyone can profit from such a map. This is correct, but we want to remember that disagreement is possible and where

disagreement is deep enough, a shared view of the landscape must acknowledge this fact.

5. *Disagreement and Sharing Maps of Value*

1. Vicious barely learned how to play, while Entwistle had the nickname "Thunderfingers" for his masterful technique. Hume's own example: "Whoever would assert an equality of genius and elegance between Ogilby and Milton, or Bunyan and Addison, would be thought to defend no less an extravagance, than if he had maintained a mole-hill to be as high as Teneriffe, or a pond as extensive as the ocean" (Hume 1987: 233, 237).

2. Proverbs often disagree among themselves: "Look before you leap," "He who hesitates is lost," "Better safe than sorry," "Nothing ventured, nothing gained" (Sagan 1996).

3. I owe a great debt in this chapter to Peter Railton's work, especially Railton (2009).

4. Judgments of value and judgments of personal preference are different in many ways. Both can be costly in many senses of the term. My claim is that an ascription of value ("X is valuable") is costlier than an ascription of personal preference ("I like X"), where the sense of "cost" is that *it takes more epistemic work* to make or defend the claim "X is valuable" than it takes to make or defend the claim "I like X."

5. Vizzini is confused about how public language works: "Fantastic" does not mean what he thinks it means. Public criteria inform the meaning of many of our words, not just value terms like "fantastic" or "tasty," but predicates expressing mind-independent properties, too—for example, "made of wool" or "north of Fargo."

6. Iris Murdoch (2001, chapter 1, "The Idea of Perfection") argues that the words we use to make moral evaluations ("vulgar," "good-hearted") are highly context-sensitive, and we learn to make better assessments the more we use moral terms in contexts where we jointly attend to the object we're evaluating.

6. *Reasonable Emotion*

1. Brady (2014) discusses several of these sources of misleading emotions and how emotions consume our attention.

2. A calm response involves some level of affect or feeling, but it falls short of full emotion, on Seneca's view (Konstan 2015).

3. Seneca believes that the fully virtuous person can feel joy, but the joy of the virtuous is not the happiness of the ordinary person (Graver 2007). It is the ordinary person—you or me—whose feelings of happiness I claim are reasonable.

4. Emotions are a heterogeneous category, in the way sand, sugar, salt, and gravel form a heterogeneous category (Scarantino and de Sousa 2021).

5. Callard ("Angry Forever") talks about what's reasonable and rational without differentiating them, so I will simplify and just consider the reasonableness of a grudge.

6. I do not have a theory of forgiveness to offer here, so I won't say where or how forgiveness emerges, except to suggest that forgiveness is also something that would be reasonable on Thursday (or later), because it also accurately tracks (some of) the valuable features of the situation as it unfolds from Monday to Thursday.

7. Reasonable Belief

1. This is what I take to be a commonsense understanding of evidence. Some philosophers prefer to work with a notion of evidence that is mentalistic: Evidence is your subjective experiences, or the propositions you know to be true. My account of reasonable belief does not depend on a particular understanding of evidence, and I offer the commonsense understanding for the reader's convenience.

2. Pinker (2021) is a good compendium.

3. (Thomson 1986, 203). For more see Tribe (1971).

4. As mentioned in Chapter 2, this is the view in Anglo-American law. One is thus liable for damages resulting from events that would have been foreseen by a reasonable person; one is accountable for grasping evidence that would have been grasped by a reasonable person, and so on.

5. I borrow the example from Gibbons (2010). Gibbons aims to defend the idea that whether our (empirical) beliefs are justified depends on factors external to our minds. He isn't concerned about the reasonableness *per se* of our beliefs. On the account I'm giving, the reasonableness of our beliefs depends on factors external to our minds (for example, such factors as whether or not some evidence was available to you).

6. This rough gloss on "available" leads to a circle: *When are you dogmatic? When you refuse to use available evidence. When is evidence available? When you can easily find it if you're not dogmatic.* Some of our concepts keep close company in this way, depending on each other for their intelligibility. The circle is only vicious if we say we're analyzing one idea ("available," say) in terms of another more fundamental idea ("dogmatism"). I'm not claiming one of these ideas is more fundamental than the other.

7. Note that on this conception of rational belief, two individuals in the same situation can differ in their beliefs and yet both have rational beliefs: "Obviously if two individuals 'have' the same evidence, in the sense of having access to the same physical objects [DNA, a smoking gun], but exactly one of them simply fails to notice a relevant piece of it, then they can rationally form different attitudes" (Kopec and Titelbaum 2016, 191).

8. *Reasonableness in Political Life*

1. I say we want a liberal democracy, though of course not all Americans want a liberal democracy—some would prefer an antidemocratic system, with an authoritarian strongman or a new "Caesar" running the show; others would prefer oligarchy, others anarchy. What do I mean, then, by "we want a liberal democracy?" Our founders articulated fundamental liberal principles, the rights of individuals to political and legal equality and liberty—freedoms of speech, religion, assembly, and more. Our constitution encodes these and other liberal principles. The constitution also encodes a guarantee to representative democracy (Article IV). Many Americans understand these rights, freedoms, and guarantees to be central to our political system and they want to preserve them. That's what I mean by "we want a liberal democracy."

2. Rawls (2005, xxiv) writes, "This pluralism is not seen as a disaster but rather as the natural outcome of the activities of human reason under enduring free institutions. To see pluralism as a disaster is to see the exercise of reason under the conditions of freedom itself as a disaster." Of course Rawls does not see the exercise of reason under conditions of freedom as a disaster—he sees it as something of great value, something to promote. Thanks to Marcia Baron for emphasizing this point.

3. Rawls calls the conditions in such cases the "burdens of judgment."

4. Political theorists disagree about whether a reasonable worldview is by definition tolerant, or whether tolerance is a further achievement. According to Samuel Freeman, it is not a constitutive requirement on the reasonableness of a worldview that it is tolerant (Freeman 2007, 350). What makes a worldview reasonable, according to Freeman, are the simple epistemic qualities of being comprehensive and being sensitive to evidence. Place such a worldview in a well-ordered society and it will tend to support toleration and liberal political principles (366–67). I am suggesting a different idea about what makes a worldview reasonable, though I am not suggesting toleration is a constitutive requirement on a reasonable worldview.

5. I have altered Rawls's official story a bit: in his thought experiment, the people who design basic principles of justice are *representatives* of those who will ultimately live in the society they design. We don't need to concern ourselves with Rawls's reasons for this wrinkle, so I drop it in giving my exposition.

6. Interested readers may consult Rawls (2001) and Voice (2011).

7. Reasonable worldviews will, Rawls hopes, overlap on basic liberal democratic principles, such as religious liberty.

8. According to Freeman (2007, 366 ff), the idea that we will reach overlapping consensus is a hopeful empirical hypothesis, one that Rawls thinks there is good reason to entertain. The hypothesis is that in a well-ordered society, our tendency to reciprocity will cultivate positive tendencies toward tolerance and liberal values. I have offered a different empirical hypothesis, based more directly on the fact that reasonable people come to understand that reasonable belief is a permissive notion.

9. Rawls emphasizes that restrictions on how we reason together apply when we argue about "constitutional essentials and questions of basic justice" such as, "who has the right to vote or what religions are to be tolerated, or who is to be assured fair equality of opportunity, or to hold property" (2005, 214).

10. Freeman (2007, 410) notes that Rawls allows that sometimes reasonable people will fail to be reasonable, and they will be unable to accept in particular instances an argument that would convince a reasonable person. But we do not have to plan around this fact.

11. Lynch (2012, 8) says that "the ideal of civility requires us to find common ground with those with whom we must discuss political matters," and finding this common ground requires some sort of agreement about basic epistemic principles. But deep disagreement about such principles is

possible, so we face a "problem of defending our epistemic principles from a common point view" (2012, p. 8). See also Kappel (2012). For more about deep disagreement see Ranalli and Lagewaard (2022).

12. Rawls (2005, lecture 2.4) says, "I assume these methods to be familiar from common sense and to include the procedures and conclusions of science and social thought, when these are well established and not controversial."

13. You might ask, "But doesn't the dispute between Eva and Finn show that it is in fact controversial whether global warming is caused by human activity?" No. By "not controversial" Rawls means "not controversial among scientists." On a separate note, I want to add that Eva and Finn might reasonably continue to argue with each other in favor of their differing standards, even if they do not hope to change each other's mind. *Agonistic conversation* can play an important role in sharpening one's understanding of one's own position, John Stuart Mill (2011) tells us. (See *On Liberty,* chapter 2.) And, I would add, it can help convince bystanders of one's position.

9. *A Role for Reasonableness in Morality*

1. See Scanlon (1982; 1998). You could reasonably reject the principle the stranger is acting on. And I could reject it, too, as a reasonable person, even though I am not immediately affected. Reasonable third parties also need to be satisfied about the justifiability of the act.

2. Scanlon (1998, 224ff) adds that the alternative Rescue Principle survives the test of reasonable rejection. The stranger on the shore might want to reject this principle, but it would be unreasonable for him to do so.

3. Does Contractualism demand that you and the stranger argue it out about principles while you are struggling in the icy lake? No, Scanlon says, discourse can help one understand others' viewpoints, but it is not what determines the rightness or wrongness of one's action (1998, 395 n18). Scanlon notes we need to distinguish "the activity of actual justification to others," and "the ideal of acting in a way that is justifi*able* to them" (1998, 168).

4. As always, different things matter depending on the particulars of one's situation. A person may have good reason for not wanting to go on, and generic reasons for rescue, while genuine reasons, may not reflect all that matters in a person's situation.

5. Scanlon proposes that the aspiration to treat people in ways justifiable to them (that is, on terms no one could reasonably reject) is a proper response to their value as persons (1998, 103–7, 168–69).

6. See also (Scanlon 2010) especially chapter 4. Scanlon talks about justifying actions to others on grounds no one could reasonably reject—a double negative he introduces to block a particular kind of counterexample. We'll ignore this nicety and reformulate his central claim as a positive one.

7. For more about this challenge to Contractualism, see R. J. Wallace (2002, 454ff).

8. Scanlon thinks this is a deep fact about human beings that gives us reason to search for mutual agreement on moral principles: humans have a distinctive value. If you recognize this value and respond appropriately you will seek to respect humans. Respecting humans means aiming to treat them in ways that are justifiable to them (Scanlon 1998, 103–7, 168–69). There is also value in this way of living (162). Is it better to be hauled out of a lake by someone who does it grudgingly (for the good publicity, say) or someone who sees your value as a human being? Who cares, you might say, so long as I'm on dry land. As for the stranger on shore, when he comes around to being reasonable and throws you the lifesaver, his life goes better.

10. Polarized Belief

1. Stanovich calls it the tragedy of the "information commons," while others favor the "communications commons," the "scientific communications commons," or "the risk-perception commons" (D. Kahan et al. 2011). I use "epistemic commons" as the more general term.

2. Kahan (2012) focuses on polarization that is rational in a practical sense of "rational": it might be good for one to believe as one's peers believe as a way to ensure smooth social relations. I set this source of polarization aside here, because it is epistemically irrational; we can free ourselves from it by being more epistemically rational.

3. Bullock writes, "Bayesian learning is compatible with the polarization of attitudes and beliefs—even when people receive the same information and interpret it in the same way." Bullock has a proof that "Even when partisans receive the same information and interpret it in the same way, Bayesian updating will lead them to agreement only if the information is of extraordinary quantity or quality" (2009, 1122). In cases where one must

evaluate the reliability of one's sources, or where the evidence before one is messy, the rationality of relying on one's priors makes myside bias rational.

4. Sides (2015) quoted in Mandelbaum (2019).

5. Favoring a hypothesis because you want it to be true is a bad epistemic habit. Kunda (1990) calls this "directed motivated reasoning." Somewhat confusingly, Stanovich's first definition of "myside bias" in his book equates it with motivated reasoning: "Myside bias occurs when we search for and interpret evidence in a manner that tends to favor the hypothesis *we want to be true*." (Stanovich 2021a, 7, my emphasis). But favoring a hypothesis because you want it to be true is irrational, whereas "myside bias" is supposed to be rational (that's what makes for tragedy). Later in his book Stanovich drops his earlier definition of "myside bias" and holds that it occurs simply when we "let prior beliefs become implicated in the process of evaluating new information" (32). Defined thus, myside reasoning is a useful epistemic habit, and you don't have to want a claim to be true to engage in myside reasoning. Still later Stanovich calls "myside bias" something more like the social identity-preserving habits of reasoning that Dan Kahan (2012) studies, writing "[myside bias] is thinking in ways that bolster one's own group or social connections" (Stanovich 2021a, 125). In this chapter I leave aside such *social identity-preserving habits* of belief formation, as an alternative source of polarized beliefs that is possibly *practically* rational, but not *epistemically* rational. I'm interested in this chapter only in polarized beliefs that arise from *epistemically rational* belief-forming practices.

6. See Herring and Lindsey (2022). Also see the Intergovernmental Panel on Climate Change 2023 report.

7. Baron suggests actively open-minded thinking reduces myside bias, but what he calls "myside bias" is failing to search for evidence against favored beliefs or hypotheses, or failing to give adequate weight to evidence against favored beliefs or hypotheses when it is available. This is different than what Stanovich means by "myside bias" in the central portion of his book.

8. The real-life Chip Kahn might reject equal opportunity, but in a liberal democracy, citizens are committed to equality of opportunity and freedom, so let's imagine instead that Chip rejects a different premise.

9. We're assuming that as reasonable people, both Chip and Bernie will strive to meet public standards in their reasoning together. That means they will respect "plain truths now widely accepted, or available, to citizens generally," as Rawls says—including the uncontroversial conclusions of science.

11. The Past and Future of Reasonableness

1. For an explanation, see John Dunbar (2012).

2. Thanks to David Hills for helpful discussion of Mill's views on freedom of speech.

3. Some political theorists who study deliberative democracy argue that we should make no appeals to emotion whatsoever in our political deliberations (Neblo 2020). But that is an extreme view. Moral philosopher Susan Okin (1989, 246) argues that both empathy and caring are required at the first stages of Rawls's imagined exercise where we hammer out the rules for a democratic system: ". . . we must develop considerable capacities for empathy" as well as "a great commitment to benevolence; to caring about each and every other as much as about ourselves." For example, empathy arguably aids our public reasoning. If I can empathize with your position as a factory worker or a doctor, I will be better at producing arguments for laws and policies that you might accept. Being concerned as a reasonable person to get it right about how things look from others' points of view is key to the fairness of these principles, and a reasonable person may rely on empathy to learn about how things are for other people. Martha Nussbaum (2004a) notes that emotions are "essential to law and to public principles of justice"—for instance, "anger at wrongdoing" is very like fear for one's safety or compassion for the pain of others—and says, "all these are good reasons to make laws that protect people in their rights." Contrast Morrell (2010).

4. (Rawls 1998, 771). Rawls does not argue against whipping up your side into action or stoking your fellow partisans with emotions so they show up at the polls, say. But he does think it would be better overall if we showed restraint even here.

5. Interestingly, Nussbaum argues that disgust is different in this respect: "Unlike anger, disgust does not provide the disgusted person with a set of reasons that can be used for the purposes of public argument and public persuasion." Why not? Because moral disgust is, according to Nussbaum, irrational: "Its cognitive content involves a shrinking from contamination that is associated with a human desire to be non-animal" (2004a). Whether Nussbaum is correct about disgust is open to debate. It seems that moral disgust often arises for reasons that are themselves fit for use in public deliberation.

6. We have various means of identifying the reasons that ground our reasonable emotions. One possible route lies in an epistemically respectable kind of rationalization. In epistemically bad rationalization, one invents

reasons for feeling as one does, solely to make one's emotion seem rational even though it is not. Othello is jealous, and his jealousy is unfounded, so he rationalizes it by inventing reasons to be jealous. This is a bad epistemic practice. But rationalization can be done well and have good epistemic effects. Fiery Cushman (2020) suggests that rationalization can help one dredge up information hidden in subpersonal cognitive systems. Peter Railton (2020), extending Cushman's idea, suggests that rationalization can help us discover the evaluative information that is buried in our emotional responses. I would add that if rationalization is governed by reasonable dispositions, we can use it to identify good reasons for our reasonable emotions—reasons which in turn will be better candidates for public deliberation.

References

Alston, William P. 1988. "An Internalist Externalism." *Synthese* 74 (3): 265–83. https://doi.org/10.1007/BF00869630.

Anderson, Elizabeth. 1995. *Value in Ethics and Economics*. Reprint, Harvard University Press.

Arendt, Hannah. 2006. *Eichmann in Jerusalem: A Report on the Banality of Evil*. Penguin Classics.

Baron, Jonathan. 2023. *Thinking and Deciding*. 5th ed. Cambridge University Press.

Ben-Ze'ev, Aaron. 1990. "Envy and Jealousy." *Canadian Journal of Philosophy* 20 (4): 487–516. https://doi.org/10.1080/00455091.1990.10716502.

Bloom, Paul. 2023. "Envy and how to defeat it." *Small Potatoes* (blog). November 12. https://smallpotatoes.paulbloom.net/p/the-worst-of-the-deadly-sins.

Bowles, Samuel. 2016. *The Moral Economy: Why Good Incentives Are No Substitute for Good Citizens*. Yale University Press.

Brady, Michael S. 2014. *Emotional Insight: The Epistemic Role of Emotional Experience*. Oxford University Press.

Bravetti, Alessandro, and Pablo Padilla. 2018. "An Optimal Strategy to Solve the Prisoner's Dilemma." *Scientific Reports* 8 (1): 1948. https://doi.org/10.1038/s41598-018-20426-w.

Bullock, John G. 2009. "Partisan Bias and the Bayesian Ideal in the Study of Public Opinion." *The Journal of Politics* 71 (3): 1109–24. https://doi.org/10.1017/S0022381609090914.

Callard, Agnes. 2020. "Angry Forever." *Boston Review*. April 16. https://www.bostonreview.net/forum/agnes-callard-philosophy-anger/.

Cancryn, Adam. 2019. "The Army Built to Fight 'Medicare for All.'" *Politico*. November 25. https://www.politico.com/news/agenda/2019/11/25/medicare-for-all-lobbying-072110.

Chiari, Mike. 2022. "Red Sox's Chris Sale Damages Locker Room on Video After Injury Rehab Start." *Bleacher Report*. July 7. https://bleacherreport.com/articles/10041236-red-soxs-chris-sale-damages-locker-room-on-video-after-injury-rehab-start.

Citizens United v. Federal Election Commission. 558 U.S. 310 (2010).

Cochrane, John. 2015. "Homo economicus or homo paleas?" *The Grumpy Economist* (blog). May 22. https://johnhcochrane.blogspot.com/2015/05/homo-economicus-or-homo-paleas.html.

Cushman, Fiery. 2020. "Rationalization is Rational." *Behavioral and Brain Sciences* 43:e28. https://doi.org/10.1017/S0140525X19001730.

Dunbar, John. 2012. "The 'Citizens United' decision and why it matters." The Center for Public Integrity. October 18. https://publicintegrity.org/politics/the-citizens-united-decision-and-why-it-matters/.

Finkel, Eli J., Christopher A. Bail, Mina Cikara, et al. 2020. "Political Sectarianism in America." *Science* 370 (6516): 533–36. https://doi.org/10.1126/science.abe1715.

Forell, Caroline. 2010. "What's Reasonable? Self-Defense and Mistake in Criminal and Tort Law." *Lewis & Clark Law Review* 14 (4): 1401–34. https://ssrn.com/abstract=1668953.

Franklin, Benjamin. 1976. *The Papers of Benjamin Franklin, Volume 19: January 1 through December 31, 1772*. Edited by William B. Willcox. Yale University Press.

Freeman, Samuel. 2007. *Rawls*. Routledge.

Gardner, John. 2001. "The Mysterious Case of the Reasonable Person." SSRN Scholarly Paper. Rochester, NY. https://papers.ssrn.com/abstract=1397115.

——. 2019a. "Reasonable Person Standard." In *The International Encyclopedia of Ethics*. John Wiley & Sons. https://doi.org/10.1002/9781444367072.wbiee920.

——. 2019b. "The Many Faces of the Reasonable Person." In *Torts and Other Wrongs*. Oxford University Press. https://doi.org/10.1093/oso/9780198852940.003.0009.

Gardner, John, and Timothy Macklem. 2004. "Reasons." In *The Oxford Handbook of Jurisprudence and Philosophy of Law*, edited by Jules L. Coleman, Kenneth Einar Himma, and Scott J. Shapiro. Oxford University Press. https://doi.org/10.1093/oxfordhb/9780199270972.013.0011.

Gerken, Mikkel. 2022. *Scientific Testimony: Its Roles in Science and Society*. Oxford University Press.

Gibbons, John. 2010. "Things That Make Things Reasonable." *Philosophy and Phenomenological Research* 81 (2): 335–61. https://doi.org/10.1111/j.1933-1592.2010.00373.x.

Gidron, Noam, James Adams, and Will Horne. 2020. *American Affective Polarization in Comparative Perspective*. Elements in American Politics. Cambridge University Press. https://doi.org/10.1017/9781108914123.

Goldie, Peter. 2008. "Misleading Emotions." In *Epistemology and Emotions*, edited by Georg Brun, Ulvi Doguoglu, and Dominique Kuenzle. Ashgate Publishing Company.

Golding, Bruce. "Rudy Giuliani asked me to cancel election so he'd stay mayor post-9/11: Pataki." 2020. *New York Post*. February 26.

Gordon, Jill. 1997. "John Stuart Mill and the 'Marketplace of Ideas." *Social Theory and Practice* 23 (2): 235–49. https://doi.org/10.5840/soctheorpract199723210.

Graver, Margaret. 2007. *Stoicism and Emotion*. University of Chicago Press. https://web.p.ebscohost.com/ehost/ebookviewer/ebook?sid=b92877ae-b395-42e4-8727-fa72c6a88307%40redis&vid=0&format=EB.

Grossmann, Igor, Richard P. Eibach, Jacklyn Koyama, and Qaisar B. Sahi. 2020. "Folk Standards of Sound Judgment: Rationality Versus

Reasonableness." *Science Advances* 6 (2): 1–14. https://doi.org/10.1126/sciadv.aaz0289.

Hart, H. L. A. 1997. *The Concept of Law*. 2nd ed. Oxford University Press.

Hattori v. Peairs. 662 So. 2d 509 (La. Ct. App. 1995). https://casetext.com/case/hattori-v-peairs.

Hawkins, Stephen, Daniel Yudkin, Míriam Juan-Torres, and Tim Dixon. 2018. "Hidden Tribes: A Study of America's Polarized Landscape." More in Common. https://hiddentribes.us/.

Helm, Bennett. 2014. "Emotional Communities of Respect." In *Collective Emotions*, edited by Christian von Scheve and Mikko Salmella. Oxford University Press.

Herbert, A. P. 1935. *Uncommon Law: Being Sixty-Six Misleading Cases Revised and Collected in One Volume*. Methuen.

Herring, David and Rebecca Lindsey. 2022. "What evidence exists that Earth is warming and that humans are the main cause?" Climate.gov. October 12. https://www.climate.gov/news-features/climate-qa/what-evidence-exists-earth-warming-and-humans-are-main-cause.

Holmes, Oliver Wendell. 2009. *The Common Law*. Reprint, Belknap Press.

Huang, Li. 2013. "Why Everybody Trusted Madoff." *Forbes*. June 19.

Hume, David. 1987. *Essays, Moral, Political, and Literary*. Liberty Classics.

Iyengar, Shanto, Yphtach Lelkes, Matthew Levendusky, Neil Malhotra, and Sean J. Westwood. 2019. "The Origins and Consequences of Affective Polarization in the United States." *Annual Review of Political Science* 22: 129–46. https://doi.org/10.1146/annurev-polisci-051117-073034.

Kahan, Dan M. 1999. "The Progressive Appropriation of Disgust." In *The Passions of Law*, edited by Susan Bandes. Critical America. New York University Press.

Kahan, Dan. 2012. "Why We Are Poles Apart on Climate Change." *Nature* 488 (7411): 255. https://doi.org/10.1038/488255a.

Kahan, Dan, Maggie Wittlin, Ellen Peters, et al. 2011. "The Tragedy of the Risk-Perception Commons: Culture Conflict, Rationality Conflict, and Climate Change." *Temple University Legal Studies Research Paper,* January. https://doi.org/10.2139/ssrn.1871503.

Kant, Immanuel. (1790) 1964. *Critique of Judgement.* Translated by J. H. Bernard. Hafner Publishing.

Kappel, Klemens. 2012. "The Problem of Deep Disagreement." *Discipline Filosofiche* 22 (2): 7–25.

Kolnai, Aurel. 1961. "Deliberation Is of Ends." *Proceedings of the Aristotelian Society* 62:195–218. https://doi.org/10.1093/aristotelian/62.1.195.

Konstan, David. 2015. "Senecan Emotions." In *The Cambridge Companion to Seneca,* edited by Shadi Bartsch and Alessandro Schiesaro. Cambridge University Press.

Kopec, Matthew, and Michael G. Titelbaum. 2016. "The Uniqueness Thesis." *Philosophy Compass* 11 (4): 189–200. https://doi.org/10.1111/phc3.12318.

Kornblith, Hilary. 1993. *Inductive Inference and Its Natural Ground: An Essay in Naturalistic Epistemology.* Bradford Books.

Krugman, Paul. 2007. "Who Was Milton Friedman?" *New York Review of Books.* February 15.

Kunda, Ziva. 1990. "The Case for Motivated Reasoning." *Psychological Bulletin* 108 (3): 480–98. https://doi.org/10.1037/0033-2909.108.3.480.

Lee, Cynthia. 2003. *Murder and the Reasonable Man: Passion and Fear in the Criminal Courtroom.* New York University Press.

Levenson, Eric and Lauren Del Valle. 2023. "College admissions scam mastermind sentenced to 3.5 years in federal prison." CNN. January 4. https://www.cnn.com/2023/01/04/us/william-rick-singer-sentencing-college-admissions-scandal/index.html.

Levy, Neil. 2022. *Bad Beliefs: Why They Happen to Good People.* Oxford University Press.

Lloyd, Lisa. 2006. *The Case of the Female Orgasm: Bias in the Science of Evolution.* Harvard University Press.

Longino, Helen. 1990. *Science as Social Knowledge: Values and Objectivity in Scientific Inquiry.* Princeton University Press.

Lord, Charles G., Lee Ross, and Mark R. Lepper. 1979. "Biased Assimilation and Attitude Polarization: The Effects of Prior Theories on Subsequently Considered Evidence." *Journal of Personality and Social*

Psychology 37 (11): 2098–2109. https://doi.org/10.1037/0022-3514.37.11.2098.

Lynch, Michael. 2012. *In Praise of Reason: Why Rationality Matters for Democracy.* MIT Press.

Mandelbaum, Eric. 2019. "Troubles with Bayesianism: An Introduction to the Psychological Immune System." *Mind & Language* 34 (2): 141–57. https://doi.org/10.1111/mila.12205.

Mill, John Stuart. 2011. *On Liberty.* Edited by Christopher Weyant and Martin Pettit. Project Gutenberg. https://www.gutenberg.org/files/34901/34901-h/34901-h.htm.

Miller, Michael. 2021. "The Pizzagate gunman is out of prison. Conspiracy theories are out of control." *Seattle Times.* February 17.

Moran, Mayo. 2003. *Rethinking the Reasonable Person: An Egalitarian Reconstruction of the Objective Standard.* Oxford University Press.

Morrell, Michael E. 2010. *Empathy and Democracy: Feeling, Thinking, and Deliberation.* Illustrated ed. Penn State University Press.

Murdoch, Iris. 2001. *The Sovereignty of Good.* 2nd ed. Routledge.

Nagel, Thomas. 1971. "The Absurd." *Journal of Philosophy* 68 (20): 716–27. https://doi.org/10.2307/2024942.

Neblo, Michael A. 2020. "Impassioned Democracy: The Roles of Emotion in Deliberative Theory." *American Political Science Review* 114 (3): 923–27. https://doi.org/10.1017/S0003055420000210.

Nesson, Charles R. 1979. "Reasonable Doubt and Permissive Inferences: The Value of Complexity." *Harvard Law Review* 92 (6): 1187. https://doi.org/10.2307/1340444.

Nussbaum, Martha. 2004a. "Discussing Disgust: On the folly of gross-out public policy. An interview with Martha Nussbaum." Interview by Julian Sanchez. *Reason Magazine.* July 15. https://reason.com/2004/07/15/discussing-disgust-2/.

———. 2004b. *Hiding from Humanity: Disgust, Shame, and the Law.* Princeton University Press. http://www.jstor.org/stable/j.ctt7sf7k.

O'Connor, Cailin. 2023. *Modelling Scientific Communities.* Cambridge Core. Cambridge University Press. November 30. https://doi.org/10.1017/9781009359535.

Okin, Susan Moller. 1989. "Reason and Feeling in Thinking about Justice." *Ethics* 99 (2): 229–49. https://doi.org/10.1086/293064.

Patchett, Ann. 2021. "Flight Plan." *New Yorker.* July 26.

Pettit, Philip. 2000. "A Consequentialist Perspective on Contractualism." *Theoria* 66 (3): 228–45. https://doi.org/10.1111/j.1755-2567.2000.tb01165.x.

Pinker, Steven. 2021. *Rationality: What It Is, Why It Seems Scarce, Why It Matters.* Viking.

Railton, Peter. 2009. "Internalism for Externalists." *Philosophical Issues* 19:166–81. https://doi.org/10.1111/j.1533-6077.2009.00165.x.

———. 2020. "Rationalization of Emotion Is Also Rational." *The Behavioral and Brain Sciences* 43 (April):e43. https://doi.org/10.1017/S0140525X19002292.

Ranalli, Chris, and Thirza Lagewaard. 2022. "Deep Disagreement (Part 1): Theories of Deep Disagreement." *Philosophy Copass* 17 (12): e12886. https://doi.org/10.1111/phc3.12886.

Rawls, John. 1998. "John Rawls on Public Reason and Discourse: An Interview." Interview by Jude Huntz. *Commonweal.* September 25. https://www.commonwealmagazine.org/interview-john-rawls.

———. 1999. *A Theory of Justice.* 2nd ed. Belknap Press.

———. 2001. *Justice as Fairness: A Restatement.* Edited by Erin I. Kelly. 2nd ed. Belknap Press.

———. 2005. *Political Liberalism.* Expanded edition. Columbia University Press.

Raz, Joseph. 1988. *The Morality of Freedom.* First paperback edition. Oxford University Press.

Reddit. n.d. "Reddit, what is the most unreasonable thing an employer has asked you to do?" Accessed October 21, 2023. https://www.reddit.com/r/AskReddit/comments/6dgirq/serious_reddit_what_is_the_most_unreasonable/?rdt=42051.

Redmayne, Mike. 2008. "Exploring the Proof Paradoxes." *Legal Theory* 14 (4): 281–309. https://doi.org/10.1017/S1352325208080117.

Rini, Regina. 2017. "Fake News and Partisan Epistemology." *Kennedy Institute of Ethics Journal* 27 (2): 43–64. https://doi.org/10.1353/ken.2017.0025.

Rouvalis, Christina. 2006. "Risk-taking can be a two-faced monster." *Pittsburgh Post-Gazette*. June 14.

Rozin, Paul, and April E. Fallon. 1987. "A Perspective on Disgust." *Psychological Review* 94 (1): 23–41. https://doi.org/10.1037/0033-295X.94.1.23.

Sagan, Carl. 1996. *The Demon-Haunted World: Science as a Candle in the Dark*. Random House.

Scanlon, T. M. 1982. "Contractualism and Utilitarianism." In *Utilitarianism and Beyond*, edited by Amartya Sen and Bernard Williams. Cambridge University Press. https://doi.org/10.1017/CBO9780511611964.007.

———. 1998. *What We Owe to Each Other*. Belknap Press.

———. 2010. *Moral Dimensions: Permissibility, Meaning, Blame*. Reprint, Belknap Press.

———. n.d. "An Interview with T. M. Scanlon (Part II)." Interview by Yascha Mounk. *The Utopian* (blog). https://www.the-utopian.org/T.M.-Scanlon-Interview-2.

Scarantino, Andrea, and Ronald de Sousa. 2021. "Emotion." In *The Stanford Encyclopedia of Philosophy* (Summer 2021 Edition), edited by Edward N. Zalta. https://plato.stanford.edu/archives/sum2021/entries/emotion/.

Scheffler, Samuel. 2011. "Valuing." In *Reasons and Recognition: Essays on the Philosophy of T. M. Scanlon*, edited by R. Jay Wallace, Rahul Kumar, and Samuel Freeman. Oxford University Press.

Seneca, Lucius Annaeus. 1900. "Of Anger." In *Minor Dialogues Together with the Dialogue On Clemency*, Book III, Section XXXIV. Translated by Aubrey Stewart. London: George Bell and Sons.

Shapiro, Barbara J. 1991. *Beyond Reasonable Doubt and Probable Cause: Historical Perspectives on the Anglo-American Law of Evidence*. University of California Press.

Sharpe, Maddie, and Alison Spencer. 2022. "Many Americans say they have shifted their priorities around health and social activities during COVID-19." Pew Research Center. August 18. https://www.pewresearch.org/short-reads/2022/08/18/many-americans-say-they-have-shifted-their-priorities-around-health-and-social-activities-during-covid-19/.

Sides, Hampton. 2015. *In the Kingdom of Ice: The Grand and Terrible Polar Voyage of the USS Jeannette*. Reprint edition. Vintage.

Stanovich, Keith E. 2021a. *The Bias That Divides Us: The Science and Politics of Myside Thinking.* MIT Press.

———. 2021b. "A Rational Disagreement about Myside Bias." *Social Epistemology Review and Reply Collective.* December 17. https://social-epistemology.com/2021/12/17/a-rational-disagreement-about-myside-bias-keith-e-stanovich/.

State of Montana v. Rudy Stanko. 974 P.2d 1132 (1998).

State v. Schaeffer. 96 Ohio St. 215, 117 N.E. 220 (1917).

Steinhauer, Jennifer. 2001. "Giuliani Is Resolute on Extending His Term." *New York Times.* October 13.

Strawson, Peter. 1962. "Freedom and Resentment." *Proceedings of the British Academy* 48:187–211.

Sugden, Robert. 2017. "Do People Really Want to Be Nudged towards Healthy Lifestyles?" *International Review of Economics* 64 (2): 113–23. https://doi.org/10.1007/s12232-016-0264-1.

Thaler, Richard H. 2015. "Unless You are Spock, Irrelevant Things Matter in Economic Behavior." The Upshot. *New York Times.* May 8. https://www.nytimes.com/2015/05/10/upshot/unless-you-are-spock-irrelevant-things-matter-in-economic-behavior.html.

Thomson, Judith Jarvis. 1986. "Liability and Individualized Evidence." *Law and Contemporary Problems* 49 (3): 199–219. https://doi.org/10.2307/1191633.

Tomasello, Michael. 2022. *The Evolution of Agency: Behavioral Organization from Lizards to Humans.* MIT Press.

Tribe, Laurence H. 1971. "Trial by Mathematics: Precision and Ritual in the Legal Process." *Harvard Law Review* 84 (6): 1329. https://doi.org/10.2307/1339610.

Tuchman, Barbara W. 1982. *Practicing History: Selected Essays.* Random House.

United States Attorney's Office, District of Massachusetts. 2020. "California Couple in College Admissions Case Sentenced to Prison." August 21. https://www.justice.gov/usao-ma/pr/california-couple-college-admissions-case-sentenced-prison.

Vaughan v. Menlove. 3 Bing. (N.C.) 467, 132 Eng. Rep. 490 (Court of Common Pleas 1837), section 10.

Voice, Paul. 2011. *Rawls Explained: From Fairness to Utopia.* Open Court.

Waldron, Jeremy. 2010. "Vagueness and the Guidance of Action." NYU School of Law, Public Law Research Paper No. 10–81, October. https://papers.ssrn.com/sol3/papers.cfm?abstract_id=1699963.

——. 2023. *Thoughtfulness and the Rule of Law.* Harvard University Press.

Wallace, Jay. 2024. "Practical Reason." In *The Stanford Encyclopedia of Philosophy* (Spring 2020 Edition), edited by Edward N. Zalta. https://plato.stanford.edu/archives/spr2020/entries/practical-reason/.

Wallace, R. Jay. 2002. "Scanlon's Contractualism." *Ethics* 112 (3): 429–70. https://doi.org/10.1086/338481.

Warren, Mark. 2014. "Help, We're in a Living Hell and Don't Know How to Get Out." *Esquire.* October 15.

Wenar, Leif, "John Rawls." In *The Stanford Encyclopedia of Philosophy* (Summer 2021 Edition), edited by Edward N. Zalta. https://plato.stanford.edu/archives/sum2021/entries/rawls/.

White, G. Edward. 2003. *Tort Law in America: An Intellectual History.* Enlarged edition. Oxford University Press.

Whitman, James Q. 2016. *The Origins of Reasonable Doubt: Theological Roots of the Criminal Trial.* Reprint, Yale University Press.

Acknowledgments

Grateful thanks to the following people for their encouragement and support, in acts large and small: Lanier Anderson, Cale Basaraba, Johan van Bentham, Michael Bratman, Sarah Brophy, Julian Davis, Dan Friedman, Michael Friedman, Mikkel Gerken, Brian Koss, Helen Longino, Patrick Rysiew, François Schroeter, Laura Schroeter, Susanna Siegel, Elise Sugarman, and Brandon Weiss.

Heartfelt appreciation to Sam Stark and Joseph Pomp, editors at HUP, for their vision and sound guidance throughout. Thanks to Emma Ingrisani for cleaning my prose. Also, I thank the Dean of the School of Humanities at Stanford University for sabbatical support for the academic year 2022–23.

Ram Neta, Marcia Baron, Rega Wood, and Peter Railton deserve special mention. Ram and Marcia read a complete draft and offered many challenging questions and excellent suggestions. Rega gave the whole a scrupulous proofread. Peter's work has inspired me, and his trenchant comments on an earlier paper helped me develop the central ideas of this book.

I owe much to my family, especially: my late brother-in-law Steven, for many uplifting conversations about art and creative struggle; my brother Gus, whose searching mind and love of reasoning did as much as anyone to turn me toward philosophy, and whose enthusiasm for this project, well before it had any shape, has buoyed me on many occasions; my husband, David, for sharing his deep understanding of value theory and its history; and our son, Ian, who teaches me every day to be open to new things that matter.

I often find myself thinking about future generations. So this book comes with a loving dedication to the next generations of the Lawlor clan—may you find a reasonable world as you set out on your journeys, Ian, Jack, and Matt.

Index

Page numbers in italics refer to figures.